Cambridgeshire Libraries, Archives and Information Service

This book is due for return on or before the latest date shown above, but may be renewed up to three times unless it has been requested by another customer.

Books can be renewed –
in person at your local library

Cambridgeshire
County Council

Online www.cambridgeshire.gov.uk/library

Please note that charges are made on overdue books.

D1255490

Also by Dan Waddell

Fiction
The Blood Detective
Blood Atonement

Selected non-fiction

And Welcome to the Highlights: 61 Years of BBC TV Cricket
Who Do You Think You Are? The Genealogy Handbook

FIELD OF SHADOWS

Dan Waddell

CORGI BOOKS

TRANSWORLD PUBLISHERS
61–63 Uxbridge Road, London W5 5SA
www.transworldbooks.co.uk

Transworld is part of the Penguin Random House group of companies
whose addresses can be found at global.penguinrandomhouse.com

First published in Great Britain in 2014 by Bantam Press
an imprint of Transworld Publishers
Corgi edition published 2015

Photos and illustrative material used courtesy of Peter Robinson's family
and Oliver Ohmann. Every effort has been made to obtain the necessary
permissions with reference to copyright material. We apologize for any
omissions in this respect and will be pleased to make the appropriate
acknowledgements in any future edition.

A CIP catalogue record for this book
is available from the British Library.

ISBN
9780552169882

Typeset in Versailles by Kestrel Data, Exeter, Devon.
Printed and bound by CPI Group (UK) Ltd, Croydon, CR0 4YY.

Penguin Random House is committed to a sustainable future for our
business, our readers and our planet. This book is made from
Forest Stewardship Council® certified paper.

1 3 5 7 9 10 8 6 4 2

For my father, Sid Waddell (1940–2012)

CONTENTS

FIELD OF SHADOWS

PROLOGUE

BERLIN IN July 1945 was a city in ruins. Fires burned and the bodies of soldiers, civilians and horses lay rotting where they had fallen; U-Bahn tunnels had been split open by bombs and those who peered in could see towers of corpses piled on one another. People moved among the smouldering buildings and houses like ghosts, foraging and hunting for food, while the four foreign armies who now occupied their city watched them and each other warily.

On a warm summer morning, a group of British soldiers were standing at a checkpoint in West Berlin. From the rubble, five middle-aged men trudged towards them. It wasn't an uncommon sight. The majority of young men had been killed in combat or captured by the Russians on their relentless, savage march into Berlin that spring and it had become a city of women, children and old men.

As the men approached, the soldiers could see they were gaunt and underfed. Leading them was a balding, serious-looking man in his mid fifties. The officer in charge watched them carefully as they drew near.

'I wonder what this lot want?' he said.

By virtue of simply not being Russian, the British had been well received in Berlin, but they were still cautious of those seeking vengeance for the tens of thousands of tons of bombs the RAF had dropped on the city. Yet instinct told the officer this forlorn group wasn't out for revenge.

The man with the serious face nodded a greeting and

smiled. His clothes were worn and flecked with dust but his receding grey hair was slicked with pomade. The officer guessed that in another time he had probably been a man of some standing.

'Good morning,' the man said, in almost perfect English.

The British soldiers murmured a greeting in return.

'Can we help?' the officer asked, cutting to the chase.

The troops had become used to these missions, the locals shuffling from the ruins to beg for fresh water, cigarettes, medicines, some women even offering their favours in return for food – all the things a conquering army might expect from a defeated people who had endured misery and suffering.

But this request would leave him open-mouthed.

'Yes,' the man replied. 'Could we play a game of cricket against you?'

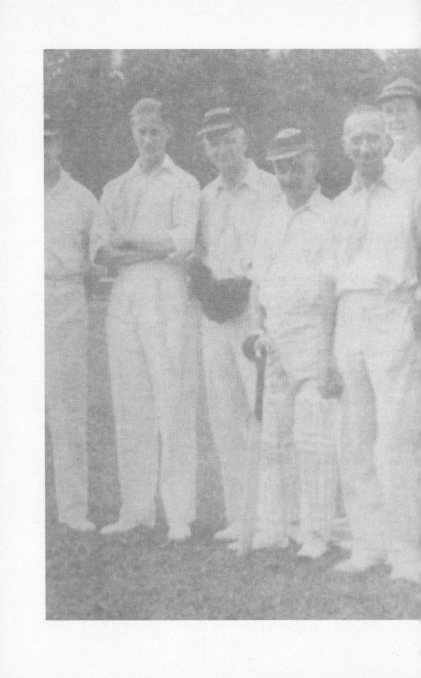

1
WHEN HITLER PLAYED CRICKET

I WAS RE-READING a collection of essays by George Orwell when the idea for this book came to me. I'd like to pretend I revisit classic works regularly, like famous writers in Sunday supplements when asked to nominate their summer reads: 'Ginny and I will be heading to Tuscany, where I hope to paint some watercolours and, as I do every year, re-read *Don Quixote*. In the original Spanish, of course.' But the truth is I was flicking through it because the only other book in the downstairs toilet was *Another Bloody Day in Paradise*, Frank Keating's wonderful account of England's troubled and tragic tour of the West Indies in 1980/81, which I've read many, many more times than any book of Orwell's.* It contains the most human account of the quirks of my boyhood hero Geoff Boycott of any book I've ever read. However, this was one of those rare times when my mind was more attracted to the thoughts of our greatest essayist than our greatest living Yorkshireman.

I had turned to 'Raffles and Miss Blandish', which Orwell

---

* I can recite chunks of it verbatim, especially the bit when David Gower, out to another flighty dismissal, asks Geoff Boycott, 'What the heck am I doing wrong, Fiery?' 'Nothing,' Boycott replies. 'That were a very good innings till you threw it away. You've got to steel yourself to concentrate every ball – *for England*. You've got to go out there and bat all day *for England*! It's not a county match out there y'know.' Re-reading that passage kept me going through the dark days of English cricket in the late 1980s and 1990s. And by God there were many of those.

wrote in 1944 in response to the increasing brutality of modern crime novels. As an occasional crime writer I found it interesting and couldn't remember reading it before. But it wasn't Orwell's sophisticated analysis of the ethics of the detective story which intrigued me. It was the bit about cricket, a game I've played since I was nine and still play now. The titular fictional hero, Raffles, was a gentleman villain. He also played cricket, which Orwell felt appropriate because it reflects something of the British character: 'In the eyes of any true cricket lover it is possible for an innings of ten runs to be better (i.e. more elegant) than an innings of a hundred runs . . .' (This is one point on which, I sense, George and Geoffrey might disagree. Violently.)

Orwell goes on, controversially, to suggest cricket was predominantly a wealthy man's game before stating, even more controversially and somewhat blithely, that 'nearly all modern-minded people dislike it'. I love Orwell and sympathize a great deal with his politics, but that comment had me muttering about dour lefties (of the political persuasion, not the Alastair Cook sort). But Orwell was setting up the next sentence – on the sort of 'modern-minded people' he was referring to. 'The Nazis, for instance, were at pains to discourage cricket, which had gained a certain footing in Germany before and after the last war.'

That sentence intrigued me. In particular the part about how cricket had flirted with popularity in Germany before being crushed under the Nazi jackboot. How did they discourage it? How popular might cricket have become in Germany if Hitler had not seized power? And *can you imagine* what life might have been like for long-suffering English cricket supporters had Germany become good at it? I always thought the swaggering, all-conquering Australia team of the 1990s and early 2000s boasted a ruthless efficiency that was almost Teutonic; the prospect of a team that actually had that quality by birthright chilled the soul.

The question 'What happened?' burrowed into my mind and never left. Finally I gave in and did what everybody does when faced with a question they can't answer: I Googled it. But it seemed the history of German cricket is like a Facebook page with original jokes on it – one of the few things you can't find on the internet. I did discover that in 1983 James D. Coldham privately published *German Cricket: A Brief History*. It was £35 – a lot of money for something with 'Brief' in the title; then again, as I went on to learn, it was one of only 125 printed. This had become an itch I needed to scratch. I decided to do what any serious cricket nerd would do – what I do when I buy bats or pads or a new helmet for my other life as a club cricketer: buy it and not tell my wife how much it cost.

The package arrived a few days later. 'Brief' seemed an adequate description: it was twenty-four pages long, so about £1.46 a page. But as it turned out, that thin green pamphlet would become the most read and well-thumbed book I've ever owned.

Serendipitously, while I scoured the internet trying to find more on German cricket and its history, and waited for my book to arrive, I stumbled across a partial answer to my question. Everyone's favourite burka-wearing war correspondent John Simpson had released a collection of newspaper reports of the twentieth century. The searches for 'Nazi + Cricket' which had previously yielded no results now linked to various news stories about an article Simpson had selected for inclusion in his book.

It had been written for the *Daily Mirror* in 1930 by Oliver Locker-Lampson, a right-wing MP and at that time a Nazi sympathizer.* It was about the Adolf Hitler he knew and admired, written to coincide with his rise to prominence in German politics. Locker-Lampson wrote that his first recollection of Hitler was 'remote and casual'. He was in southern Germany between the wars and had been discussing Hitler with some British Army officers because he was the talk of the country after the failed 'Beer Hall Putsch' of 1923, which had led to his trial and imprisonment. Some of those officers had been POWs in Germany during the First World War and had been in a military hospital as 'prisoners on parole'. The notoriously shy and socially inept Hitler had summoned up the courage to speak to them. 'He had come to them one day and asked whether he might watch an eleven of cricket at play so as to become initiated into the

---

* Locker-Lampson was a committed anti-Bolshevist whose desire to bash the Reds led him into some ill-advised partnerships. He founded the Sentinels of Empire in 1931, also known as Blue Shirts, an anti-communist group that came to Hitler's attention in the early 1930s. Once the true nature of Hitler's fascism was revealed, in particular his policy towards the Jews, Locker-Lampson turned his ire on fascism home and abroad. He opposed appeasement and was one of the few sitting Conservative MPs to support Churchill during his years in the political wilderness. Most notably, he personally sponsored the escape of ordinary Jews from persecution in Germany and Austria. He came to regard Hitler as a monster. Quite a turnaround for a man who wrote in the article mentioned here that he was a 'legendary hero'.

mysteries of our national game,' Mr Locker-Lampson wrote. 'They welcomed him, of course, and wrote out the rules for him in the best British sport-loving spirit.'

Hitler then 'vanished', only to return a few days later to announce that he had been training a team of Germans and wanted to play the English at the first opportunity. The officers agreed to a friendly match, the scores of which are unknown. But the game had a profound effect on the would-be dictator and, perhaps, the future of continental Europe and world peace. As a result of his experiences, Hitler declared the game insufficiently violent for the prime of German *Volk*. (Had he played a team of Australians, it could be argued he might have formed a different opinion.)

Its serenity aside, the Führer had several other issues with cricket. Most notably, he felt it 'unmanly and un-German' that batsmen wore pads to protect their legs – from which we can only deduce that he was never hit in the shin by a fast bowler, because he would have been a signed-up, card-carrying believer in the necessity of donning pads if he had been. As all schoolboys know, to play a front-foot drive you need to get your foot to the pitch of the ball, which is hard to do with a fractured fibula.

'He had conned over [sic] the laws of cricket, which he considered good enough no doubt for pleasure-loving English people,' wrote Mr Locker-Lampson. 'But he proposed entirely altering them for the serious-minded Teuton.' According to Locker-Lampson, Hitler's real interest in cricket was as a 'possible medium for the training of troops off duty and in times of peace'. That he found it wanting won't come as a surprise to amateur cricketers. The sport offers some useful lessons for life but it's unlikely that 'He who gets into the tea-room first gets all the best cakes' develops the necessary discipline to win wars.

But here was a clue to why Hitler and his 'modern-minded' cronies were as vehemently opposed to cricket as Orwell suggested. He had played the game, learned the rules, and decided it was not masculine enough for the German male. Over time, as his dislike for the English grew, so did his distaste for their customs and whims, cricket among them.

Of the many fascinating details James Coldham included in his book, one story stood out above all. In August 1937, with Nazism at its zenith, a touring team from England played three matches in Berlin. I was further intrigued. I have been on amateur cricket tours. With very few exceptions they are a social affair. A group of men, liberated from the responsibilities of work and family, play cricket to idle away time until it is socially acceptable to start drinking. The next day, battered and wearied by alcohol, they take to the field again. It turns into a test of endurance. Long-term friendships become as strained as the participants' livers. Close proximity to each other and industrial quantities of booze can be a combustible mix, and all manner of petty jealousies and barely concealed loathings are liable to surface. At the end of the week, the tourists crawl back home to scowling wives vowing never to repeat the experience. But the very next year they do.

Touring cricketers have often visited quirky and offbeat places. Some take pride in playing as far off the beaten track as possible, the more weird and wonderful the better, whether it's the Sahara Desert or the North Pole.* But no amateur team I know of has ever chosen to play in a country and city under the rule of a totalitarian regime. The touring team of 1937 were the Gentlemen of Worcestershire, and if they fancied a foreign field to play on they could have visited Denmark, Portugal or the Netherlands – all countries where they had played before, where there was a healthy cricket culture and a community of expats to share a cooling G&T with after play, and which weren't in the murderous grip of a crazed dictator.

Yet more Googling revealed that the Gentlemen of Worcestershire still existed. I contacted their secretary, BBC radio correspondent Phil Mackie. He told me the club dated back to the mid nineteenth century and it was formed around the same time as Worcestershire CCC by many of the same people. Ever since there had been close links between the two teams. In the days of amateurism, many Gents had played for the county and several had gone on to take administrative and honorary roles on the committee. The Worcester Gents, as they were less formally known, had enjoyed their heyday at the beginning of the twentieth century, during cricket's so-called Golden Age. The great Worcestershire cricketing families of the nineteenth and twentieth centuries, such as the Lyttletons, Berkeleys, Foleys and Fosters, had all been prominent members. Some famous names had appeared for them, including the 9th Marquess of Queensberry, who lent his name and patronage to the rules that formed the basis of modern boxing, and the Nawab of Pataudi. These days

---

* The late Harry Thompson wrote a very funny book about cricketers and cricket called *Penguins Stopped Play* in which they played at the South Pole.

the club may be less aristocratic but they still play fixtures against the great amateur teams: the Free Foresters, the Gloucestershire Gypsies and the Cryptics, as well as their counterparts, the 'Gentlemen' teams of Herefordshire and Shropshire.

The story of the tour to Berlin was news to Phil. But then, he explained, as a consequence of the team's casual, Corinthian status its history is somewhat hazy. The club had just celebrated its 150th anniversary . . . only for Phil to do some research and discover it was actually 160 years old. He was delighted by my discovery. True to form as the administrative honcho of a nomadic team, he immediately started planning a tour to Berlin for the current Gents. But for me he had no information other than a few names of some former players to write to.

Thanks to Coldham I had a short summary of the scores and a brief account of each match. There were no other books to consult, no more websites to search. An email to the German cricket authorities drew a blank. If I was to find out any more about this fascinating tour – and by now the urge was all-consuming – I would have to dig it out myself.

In a doctor's waiting room one weekday morning I picked up a glossy magazine to idle away a few minutes. Flicking through it I came across a photoshoot featuring the model Rosie Huntington-Whiteley. She was wearing very little clothing. My reaction reminded me of the time I was walking through west London and saw Mike Atherton pushing his son in an expensive three-wheeled buggy. I didn't think,

'There's former England captain and gritty opener Mike Atherton.' I'd just become a new father and was still in a state of shock at the complete obliteration of my previous life and all its interests. So I thought, 'Nice pushchair.' Likewise, gazing at Rosie's flawless figure draped suggestively over a chair I didn't contemplate her obvious beauty, I thought, 'She shares a surname with one of the Worcester Gents who toured Berlin.'

By this time I had managed to find an announcement of the touring party in an edition of *Berrows Worcestershire Journal* (31 July 1937):

> I understand that a team of Worcestershire Gentlemen leaves shortly for Berlin, for 10 days cricket in the capital. Major M. F. S. Jewell will captain the team [. . .]
>
> Herr Hitler is reported to be very interested in the tour, for German cricket is still in the student stage, and there is a great desire to improve the standard of play.
>
> The team: R. G. W. Berkeley, M. F. S. Jewell, C. S. Anton, W. Deeley, G. S. Tomkinson, R. H. Williams, C. G. D. Smith, H. T. H. Foley, M. Jewell, R. Whetherly, C. Terry, P. Huntington-Whiteley, P. Robinson.

Some of these names were easier to find out about than others because, like their captain, they had played first-class cricket and cricket followers have been collecting statistics and records for decades. Major M. F. S. Jewell was Maurice Jewell, former Worcestershire captain; R. G. W. Berkeley was Robert George Wilmot Berkeley, who played four very unsuccessful matches for Worcestershire, scoring 37 runs with an average of 5.28; R. H. Williams played thirty-seven matches for the county and scored 713 runs at an un-spectacular average of 11.14. These men were amateurs who had been asked to play a few matches for their county but were palpably not good enough to succeed at that level.

H. T. H. Foley was Henry Thomas Hamilton Foley, who played a single first-class match for Worcestershire against Oxford University in 1925 and scored 6 and 0 not out. He came from the Foley family, one of the most celebrated dynasties in Worcestershire. Paul Foley was Speaker in the House of Commons at the turn of the eighteenth century. A descendant of his, also named Paul, was responsible for establishing the county cricket club in the 1880s – which might have been how Henry was able to get a game forty or so years later. Edward Foley was Lord of the Manor of Malvern during the first part of the nineteenth century, after whom the famous Foley Arms was named (the pub is now owned by another celebrated British family, Wetherspoon). But Foley is not mentioned in James Coldham's account of the matches in Berlin: it turned out he didn't go on the tour. C. G. D. Smith doesn't appear in Coldham's history either. Did he miss the tour as well? I wondered. Another newspaper report I found printed almost the identical touring party but featured one M. Mallinson instead of P. Robinson. Again, Coldham makes no mention of a Mallinson. What happened to *him*? And who were all the other names on the list?

This was why the glimpse I caught of the comely Miss Huntington-Whiteley was so welcome. Enough had been written about Rosie for me to discover that the Huntington-Whiteleys are minor aristocracy. The article announcing the touring party had given the initial 'P.', while Coldham gave 'H. O.'. Going through the Peerage, an online genealogical survey of our landed gentry, I discovered that Rosie and H. O. (not P.) were related. She was the great-great-granddaughter of Herbert Huntington-Whiteley, a former MP and the 1st Baronet of Grimley. H. O., or Herbert Oliver to give him his full name, was his grandson (and Rosie's great-great-uncle), born in 1920. There were no other H. O. Huntington-Whiteleys, which meant he was in his teens when the tour was held and still a pupil at Eton. Even more intriguingly, it turned out that Herbert was the eldest son of Captain Sir Herbert Maurice Huntington-Whiteley RN 2nd Bt and Lady Pamela Margaret Huntington-Whiteley of Astley, Stourport-on-Severn, Worcestershire. Lady Pamela's maiden name was Baldwin, and her father was Stanley Baldwin, the former British Prime Minister. He had only stepped down as PM in May 1937, exhausted by the constitutional crisis surrounding the abdication of Edward VIII the previous winter. Which meant the grandson of the former Prime Minister would be playing cricket in Hitler's Germany only weeks after his resignation – a fact which must have excited the German press.

Baldwin was not the family's only famous connection. Rudyard Kipling, whose death in 1936 together with the increasing belligerence of Hitler and the scandal of Edward and Mrs Simpson had created a pall of gloom over the entire country, had been godfather to H. O.'s younger brother Miles. There's a picture of Kipling as an elderly man sitting in a paddle boat with Miles on the lake he built at his home in Burwash, East Sussex. Miles and another brother, Hugo, were still alive. I wrote to Hugo and received a very kind response. He knew nothing about the tour but suggested that I write to a childhood friend of H. O.'s, George Chesterton.

He also revealed that his brother was known as Peter, which explained why *Berrows Journal* referred to him as P. Huntington-Whiteley.

Chesterton turned out to be three parts schoolmaster and two parts *Boys' Own* hero. He played for Worcestershire after the Second World War and took 263 wickets at 22.78 apiece with his steady seam bowling, for several decades he coached and taught cricket at the school he attended as a boy, Malvern College,* and he wrote a book on coaching young cricketers. In the Second World War he was a pilot, he danced with Katharine Hepburn while training in New York, and he narrowly escaped death during the ill-fated Battle of Arnhem, which he was to describe as a 'cauldron of hell'.

His response to my letter was polite, amusing and illuminating. He told me that an overseas tour was an annual feature of the Gents' cricketing calendar; among other places they'd been on trips to Holland, Malta and Portugal. Major Jewell ran the tour and took his son, Young Maurice, and childhood friend Peter Huntington-Whiteley, whose family was close to the Jewells.

In his final paragraph, Mr Chesterton passed on a tantalizing piece of information: 'The Huntington-Whiteleys had an early bowling machine in their conservatory. It had to be cranked up, but was amazingly accurate.' My mind boggled. First of all, how exactly did it work? Unfortunately neither of the surviving Huntington-Whiteley brothers could

---

* The school was appropriated for use by Churchill at the outbreak of the Second World War and the pupils evacuated to Blenheim Palace, where Churchill was born, and where young Chesterton was forced to apologize to the Duke of Marlborough when he broke a window in the Long Library while practising his slip catching.

remember, though Miles did tell me on the phone 'there was lots of rope attached to it', which brought to mind a Heath Robinson contraption powered by steam kettles and complex pulley arrangements. My second thought was, the conservatory?! Were the Huntington-Whiteleys so wealthy that they could afford to let their son play with a bowling machine in a room largely made of glass? Or was it a cunning way to teach a boy stout defence, knowing an attacking shot could break a window? One can imagine Geoff Boycott perfecting his forward defensive in a greenhouse.

However it worked, it appears to have helped Peter become a better cricketer. He played his way into the Eton College first XI for the 1937 season, his penultimate year at the school. Initially he didn't bowl and batted at 10, but against Marlborough he was given the new ball and took four wickets and three weeks later he was opening the bowling at Lord's in the annual match versus Harrow, at that point still one of the highlights of the English cricket calendar. The fixture's enduring popularity illustrates how cricket between the wars was still clinging to the cosy certainties of the Golden Age. The socialists might briefly have been in government, the King might have been forced to abdicate because of a fling with an American divorcee, and there might have been an embarrassing ballyhoo with the Australians over Bodyline, but no professional had yet captained England, the amateurs remained in charge of the ranks, and the Eton–Harrow match was still the game where society and cricket mingled. It is staggering to think that the 1937 fixture was the 132nd contest; the first took place a few months before the Battle of Trafalgar, and featured Lord Byron. 'Later to be sure,' Byron wrote of the post-match revelry, 'we were most of us very drunk and we went together to the Haymarket Theatre where we kicked up a row, as you may suppose when so many Harrovians and Etonians meet in one place.' Byron would not be the last part-time cricketer to be more interested in the post-match piss-up than the match itself.

Eton won in 1937, but then they always did. Their coach was George Hirst, the former Yorkshire and England all-rounder; under his tutelage the team lost only one match in eighteen years and regularly trounced Harrow. That year's game has entered history, though not for anything that happened on the field. On the first morning a press photographer passed by the Grace Gates where he saw two boys from Harrow School dressed in uniform including waistcoat, top hat, boutonnière and cane; they appeared to be studiously ignoring three smirking working-class lads to their right, all of them seemingly amused by the pair's haughty indifference. The resulting image, which became known as Toffs and Toughs, is still one of the most famous photographs in British history.

On the field, Peter Huntington-Whiteley bowled accurately and took three wickets in the match. Less than a month later he was part of Major Jewell's touring team to Berlin.

Alongside him in the party were a trio of Marlburians, among them P. N. L. Terry (mistakenly referred to as C. Terry in *Berrows Journal*), the second victim claimed by Huntington-Whiteley in the match at Marlborough earlier that season. Maurice Jewell, the son of Major Maurice Jewell, attended the school between September 1933 and July 1938 and played for the College first XI in both 1937 and 1938, though he wasn't selected for the match against Eton. But he did play at Lord's, in their annual match against Rugby, scoring 0 and 24. The following appraisal was published in *The Marlburian* in October 1938: 'His batting showed a great improvement this year. His defence was sound and he hit the ball hard, so much so that his main fault was his desire to take full advantage of his strength. He never played a big innings, but there was a long period when he always made 30s and 40s.' Rather unkindly it added, 'He did his best to overcome his natural inability as a fielder.'

Peter Noel Leetham Terry was yet another well-connected member of the Worcester Gents touring side. His family were Terry's of York, of chocolate-making fame, and Terry's father Noel had been responsible for revamping the company when he took control with his brother Frank in 1923, opening the art deco chocolate factory which loomed Wonka-like over Bishopthorpe Road in the city for decades to come. In contrast to Young Maurice's muscular style, Peter was an elegant strokemaker. He arrived at Marlborough in 1932 and made his debut in the first XI in 1935, at Lord's against Rugby. His talents weren't confined to cricket: he also played for the rugby XV in 1936 and for the hockey XI in 1937.* He made a debut century for Yorkshire Gentlemen when at home in York for the summer holidays. In July 1937 *The Marlburian* wrote this about his cricketing talents: 'A batsman of great ability, who has a sound defence and a

* It's not mentioned in his college magazine, but Terry was equally talented in individual sports. He was an excellent golfer, tennis and squash player, and a dab hand at bridge, too.

wide range of scoring strokes. He could always be relied upon to make 30 or 40 runs, but, unfortunately he never obtained the experience of a big innings to enable him to "open-out" safely, and to give him the confidence which he needed. His fielding on the boundary was often brilliant.' He was out for a duck in his last innings for the school (Rugby at Lord's again), dismissed in the same over as Maurice Jewell.

The final Marlburian to tour Berlin should have been Michael Mallinson, one of the school's most successful players between the wars, whose accurate leg-spin made him a mainstay of the bowling attack from 1936 to 1938. But for reasons unknown he was unable to go and he was replaced a few days before they travelled by P. E. B. Robinson. Mallinson had missed the final few matches of Marlborough's season, including that showpiece match at Lord's against Rugby. As the college magazine lamented his absence, we can assume he wasn't dropped and that the injury, illness or family commitment which prevented him playing also denied him the opportunity of going to Berlin.

Unlike Mallinson, according to the Marlborough archives Robinson didn't play for any of the college XIs at any sport, though he did play for his house XI (B3, the same as Terry), but without any distinction. Beyond that, little was known about him. His story intrigued me. Robinson was only sixteen yet here he was venturing off to Nazi Germany, ostensibly to make up the numbers.

By this stage of my research I had managed to find solid enough information on most of the tourists. I had only basic biographical details for C. S. Anton, W. Deeley and C. G. D. Smith but I'd been lucky to track down a number of living relatives or friends of many of the others and exchanged letters, emails and phone calls with them. I had enjoyed a fish and chip lunch with Major Jewell's grandson; visited the son of R. G. W. Berkeley at Spetchley Castle and admired the piano Don Bradman had played at a soirée during his final Ashes tour in 1948; I had also travelled through a blizzard by train and taxi to a bungalow in the hills overlooking High Wycombe where the daughter of G. S. Tomkinson, Meg Freeman, fed me cake and hot sweet tea while I leafed through the yellowing pages of her father's scrapbook.

It was there that I set eyes on the tourists for the first time, in an informal team photograph above an article in a German magazine which Tomkinson had brought back from the tour. I recognized Major Jewell immediately from images I had seen in histories of Worcestershire CC. He was in the middle, hands in front, fingers entwined, his hair combed neatly over his balding pate, swarthier than the others. As captain, he was the only player wearing a blazer. Who was who among the others remained a mystery, though Mrs Freeman did point out her father, standing insouciantly third from the left in a Worcester Gents cap and a pair of wicketkeeping gloves. Why he was keeping was another puzzle, but as he wasn't wearing pads perhaps it was only for fielding practice.

My eye was drawn to an awkward, gangly young man at the back with a geeky smile, who looked as if he was trying to hide from the camera. Who was he? I wondered. Peter Huntington-Whiteley, or one of the Marlburians? His cap was different to the green, black and purple hooped cap of the Worcester Gents worn by some of the senior players, but it was impossible to identify as an Etonian one.

The details of some of the other men involved were sketchier and more elusive, and a common theme was developing: few of them had ever spoken in detail about the tour and its events (which stoked my interest in it even further – were they in some way ashamed of having been there?). Nor was the tour covered in any detail by the British press. Rather than putting me off, this scarcity of information made me grit my teeth. It became a quest to find out more.

The most elusive were Whetherly and Robinson. Neither was a Worcester Gents regular. The first for reasons as yet unknown; the second because he too was a teenager and wasn't that good at cricket. Beyond the information sent to me from the Marlborough archives, the only lead I had on Robinson was an announcement of his death in 2005 in the *Daily Telegraph*. His full name was Peter Ellis Backhouse Robinson. He had married Eve Hinchliffe, gone on to become managing director of a cotton firm in Manchester, and lived most of his life in a village in Cheshire. I contacted the nearest cricket club to his former home, even the local pub, but no one knew him. The death notice named his children as Michael, Jilly and Henry, which made my heart sink. I've carried out enough genealogical research to know that in order to track down people with common surnames such as Robinson you need distinctive Christian names. Still, I spent hours searching for Michael and Henry Robinsons on electoral rolls, in phone books and the indexes on Ancestry with no luck (I assumed Jilly would have got married and changed her name).

In an idle moment I decided to start playing around with middle names. I dug out Peter and Eve's marriage certificate and it became clear that 'Ellis' and 'Backhouse' were family names: Ellis Robinson was an ancestor, and Backhouse was another family name on the Robinson side. In a moment of inspiration, or desperation, I did the same with Henry Robinson and searched on the internet for one Henry Peter Hinchliffe Robinson.

There was a hit in an index of company directors. I sent an email to the company asking to be put in touch with him if possible. A few days later I received an understandably cautious reply:

> You were trying to find me
> This is my email address
> Henry Robinson.

I felt the surge of excitement all researchers do when they appear to have a breakthrough. But there was still a good chance this was the wrong Henry Robinson and there seemed little point in giving him chapter and verse about the project unless he was the right one. I mentioned the cricket tour to Berlin, that I was writing a book on it, and asked whether his father was Peter Ellis Backhouse Robinson, a former pupil at Marlborough College.

> Dan
> Yes indeed he was.
> I must admit I didn't know he went on a cricket tour to
> Berlin. Sounds unlikely!
> When?
> Henry

24

In response I sent a copy of the team photo from the German magazine which I'd found among the faded clippings inside G. S. Tomkinson's scrapbook. I asked if his father was among those pictured. He replied almost immediately:

Yes, absolutely. How extraordinary.
He is the furthest right.
Now I would really like to know more!!
Thanks
Henry

We spoke on the phone for more than half an hour. He knew nothing about the tour. His father had never spoken about it. Nor was Peter much of a cricketer. However, there was a connection to the Jewells. Henry's grandfather had been in charge of a tea plantation in Ceylon and Peter had been sent to board at Marlborough. But in the mid 1930s the family had returned to England and settled in Upton-on-Severn, where they became friendly with the Jewells. Henry had a vague memory of them from a holiday spent visiting his grandparents; his older brother Michael remembered watching England playing the West Indies on the television as a child with a very elderly Major Jewell. This explained how Peter had been drafted into the tour party at such late notice. For a brief period he had also dated one of the Major's daughters.

During our phone conversation, Henry mentioned that his grandmother, known to them as 'Gun', had kept a scrapbook of her family's life and it might be worth checking to see if there was any mention in it of Peter going on the tour. A few days later he emailed to let me know there was more than just a mention: she had kept several letters Peter had sent from Berlin. Even better, there was also a scrapbook that Peter had put together with memorabilia from the trip.

This discovery was a breakthrough. It meant the story and all its characters could finally come to life.

2

DAS MEKKA

IN THE SUMMER of 1937, the Nazi Reichssportführer* Hans von Tschammer und Osten travelled to England. His visit coincided with the conclusion of the Davis Cup semi-final between Germany and the USA at Wimbledon. The previous year he had watched Australia, led by the great Jack Crawford, beat the German pair of Gottfried von Cramm and Henner Henkel 4–1 in the semi-finals and he did not want to witness another defeat. Cramm had won the first singles match but in the second Henkel was annihilated by Wimbledon champion Don Budge in straight sets in only fifty minutes. According to one spectator, quoted in Christopher Hilton's *How Hitler Hijacked World Sport*, at the moment of defeat Henkel looked towards the royal box, where Tschammer und Osten was sitting. 'Their eyes met for one pregnant moment and then I saw Henkel flinch under [Tschammer und Osten's] disdainful gaze and turn away like a dog that knows it will be whipped. It was a small incident, but frighteningly revealing and altogether alien to the sunny, smiling scenes so closely associated with lawn tennis as we like to know it here.'

Bear in mind that the Reichssportführer was regarded as one of the most charming Nazi leaders – though admittedly the competition for that description was not hotly contested. According to Ulrich Hesse-Lichtenberger in *Tor! The Story of German Football*, Tschammer und Osten 'was one of those

* Minister for Sport, essentially.

strange men German fascism either produced or was built upon. He possessed personality in spades but apparently no character.' Unlike most Nazi leaders he was clubbable and loved to spin yarns while 'downing glass after glass'. A smiling, damned villain who 'knew next to nothing about sport'.

Unlike his close friend Adolf Hitler, Tschammer und Osten was an aristocrat. He had been a leading member of the Sturmabteilung, the Nazi paramilitary force that had been instrumental in helping Hitler gain control of Germany but whose power had diminished after the 'Night of the Long Knives' on 30 June 1934. Though many SA men were imprisoned or executed on falsified charges of plotting to overthrow their Führer, most notably their leader Ernst Rohm, Tschammer und Osten had remained in a position of influence. A handsome man, his penchant for white suits and leather boots and caps meant he stood out in a crowd. He was not one for the day-to-day bureaucracy and surrounded himself with others willing to do his bidding while he channelled his energies into 'wine, women and song'.

Two days later he was back at Wimbledon. The tie stood at 2–2 with the final singles game to come, between the plain American 'Hayseed' Budge and Germany's finest player, the elegant, aristocratic Gottfried von Cramm. There was an undercurrent of irony as Tschammer und Osten took his place in the royal box at Wimbledon, the Nazi flag billowing side by side with the American Stars and Stripes above Centre Court. Cramm was the pride of German tennis and his blond hair and good looks made him the poster boy for Aryan supremacy – an embodiment of the health, power and vitality which the Nazis so passionately championed. Yet he despised Nazism. Tschammer und Osten was aware of his antipathy but was happy to use his talents as a propaganda tool.

The match has entered sporting legend. The writer James Thurber described it as 'something so close to art that at the end it was more as if a concert had ended than a tennis match'. Cramm won the first two sets with sublime tennis before Budge, fearsomely competitive and supremely fit, fought back and claimed the next two. Eventually, after a brutal final set in which both men squandered chances to win, Budge emerged the winner 6–8 5–7 6–4 6–2 8–6. At its conclusion Tschammer und Osten applauded with the rest of the enraptured Centre Court crowd, most of whom had been supporting the dashing German. But behind the smiling facade he was beginning to wonder whether Cramm was worth the effort. The Nazis loved winners but their best tennis player had now lost three Wimbledon championships and had once again failed to secure a Davis Cup for his country. This would not have mattered had Cramm been a Nazi, and had he not been carrying a secret: he was homosexual, and the Gestapo knew it. To make matters worse, his lover was Jewish. Cramm needed to keep winning to avoid prosecution, ruin or worse. It's no exaggeration to say he was playing for his life. Even though he and Budge became the toast of the tennis world for producing such an epic encounter, the loss would have terrible consequences for Cramm.

Tschammer und Osten had another week to spend in England after the tennis. Next he attended the British Athletics Championship at the White City Stadium. While German athletes had little success on the track, they managed to win several field events, among them Luz Long in the long jump. Long had finished second in the Berlin Olympics to Jesse Owens, the black American athlete whose success and popularity with the home crowd had been the only blight on the Games for the Nazis.

After a visit to a swimming competition between Germany and England at Wembley, which appears to have gone unrecorded and unreported, the remainder of the Reichssportführer's tour was taken up with selling the Nazi brand to interested parties in England. He gave a talk at the German Embassy about physical education in his home country, interspersed with clips from Leni Riefenstahl's forthcoming epic about the Berlin Games, *Olympia*, and followed that with a visit to the German Sports Group in London. By invitation from Brigadier General Andrew Thorne he visited the Army School of Physical Training in Aldershot. Thorne, a decorated First World War veteran, had been military attaché to the British Embassy in Berlin between 1932 and 1935 and during that time had got to know many of the Nazi leaders, including Hitler. Both the German leader and Thorne had fought at Gheluvelt in 1914 and had shared their experiences with each other at length.

Next on Tschammer und Osten's itinerary was a tea reception held by the Anglo-German Fellowship, followed by a dinner at Claridge's as guest of the newly formed National Fitness Council, a body set up to promote health and well-being among the British population. His hosts were Lord Aberdare and Lord Portal. Aberdare, who as Clarence Bruce played ninety-six first-class matches for Middlesex between 1908 and 1929, was the Council's chairman; he also served on the International Olympic Committee and would organize the 1948 London Olympics. Lord Portal was Charles Portal, then Air Vice Marshal of the RAF, who three years into the future would mastermind Britain's response to the Blitzkrieg launched by Tschammer und Osten's Nazi confrères. Also present was Lord Burghley, aka David Burghley, Conservative MP for Peterborough and a gold medallist in the 400m hurdles at the 1928 Olympics. Perhaps his greatest achievement had come the year before, in his final year at Cambridge, when he sprinted around the Great Court at Trinity College in the time it took the college clock to toll twelve o'clock – which became the inspiration for the famous scene in *Chariots of Fire* in which Harold Abrahams accomplishes the same feat racing against Lord Andrew Lindsay, whose character was based on Burghley. In reality Abrahams never achieved the feat and Burghley was never beaten, which is why he didn't allow his name to be used in the film.

As these personalities suggest, Tschammer und Osten was courted by some of the most pre-eminent names in British sport. Throughout his stay he was a guest of Oliver Hoare, the president of Wimbledon. Hoare's brother was Samuel, the former Home Secretary who had resigned in 1935 following Mussolini's invasion of Abyssinia (Ethiopia). In a pact with the French Prime Minister, Hoare had agreed to grant the Italians concessions in Abyssinia as an act of appeasement, aiming to dissuade Mussolini from forming an alliance with his fellow fascist Hitler. The plan was an abysmal failure: the Italians seized control of the entire country and forged an even closer relationship with Germany, a partnership which would have disastrous consequences for Europe and the world.

The Reichssportführer's published itinerary did not

include cricket, but the minutes of the MCC Committee reveal that on 23 July Hans von Tschammer und Osten did visit Lord's. There he was 'entertained to lunch' and watched 'Big' Jim Smith take five wickets as Middlesex bowled Worcestershire out for 153 and a defeat by 214 runs.* Any cricket lover who has been fortunate enough to visit Lord's will understand the seductive scene the Reichssportführer faced. Gazing across the most famous ground in the world from the committee dining room on the top floor of the pavilion, one's belly sated, watching Big Jim blow away the brittle Worcestershire batting as the sun bathed the ground would have been enough to melt the hardest of hearts – and be sure that Tschammer und Osten's heart was as hard as they come despite the bluff and clubbable veneer. He was also a member of the German landed gentry, and in that dining room he was in the company of men he would have considered of good breeding. The MCC was then, as now, hardly a nest of Bolshevism, so it's unlikely he overheard too many opinions he disagreed with. Perhaps, his lips loosened by the wine he so enjoyed and basking in a post-prandial glow, he might well have let slip a white lie about his Führer and close friend's admiration of cricket, a tidbit eagerly snapped up by chairman of selectors Sir Pelham Warner and the other guests? Maybe the panjandrums of the MCC warmed to this

---

* The very next day, after bowling an unbroken spell of twenty-one overs to skittle Worcestershire, Jim Smith played a Test match for England against New Zealand at Old Trafford (no resting of bowlers back then). He bowled thirty-six overs in the match, took four wickets for just sixty-three runs and never played another Test in his life. Big Jim was also a big-hitting batsman: he once scored a fifty in eleven minutes against Gloucestershire and hit a six that cleared the Old Grandstand at Lord's.

suave, jovial man who undermined the commonly held view that most Nazis were vulgar oiks?

When he returned to Berlin Tschammer und Osten wrote a report for his beloved Führer which carries written confirmation that Hitler read it. In it Tschammer und Osten claimed that his visit strengthened Germany's sporting relationship with England, and he drew a disparaging comparison between the various British 'boys' clubs' he was taken to see and the 'wholesome care and education provided to every boy and girl' in the Hitler Youth. In contrast, Lord's had made a favourable impression. 'This is the so-called "Mekka" of English cricket,' he rhapsodized.

It appears likely that the idea of a tour to Berlin was hatched in that committee dining room at Lord's. However, according to James Coldham it was during his visit to England the previous year, before the 1936 Olympics, that Tschammer und Osten watched some cricket and was said to be so impressed that when he returned to Berlin for the Games he 'drew the attention of the sports-attachés and journalists of cricket-playing countries at the Olympic Games to the Berlin Cricket League and sent personal invitations to various clubs to visit Berlin on cricket tours'.

One of those invitations arrived on the MCC's mat at Lord's, where it came to the attention of Sir Pelham Warner. 'Plum' Warner was not only chairman of selectors, he was a former England captain, current editor of *The Cricketer* magazine, and the pre-eminent cricket administrator of his time, though these days he is probably most remembered for his spinelessness as MCC tour manager during the infamous Bodyline series in Australia in 1932/33. He mulled over the invitation before deciding it might be a good idea to give it to Major Maurice Jewell, the captain of the Gentlemen of Worcestershire and an acquaintance of Warner's: the pair had been on an MCC tour to South America together in 1926/27, and Warner had stayed as a guest at Jewell's house, The Hill in Upton-on-Severn, on several occasions. The Major accepted the invitation and the tour was on.

But the record indicates something rather less organized. The archives of the Deutsche Reichsbund für Leibesübungen (or DRL, the Nazi Ministry for Sport) were destroyed during the war so there is no record of the invitation sent to the MCC or any response. Neither is there anything in the MCC's archives at Lord's. If the tour had been arranged a year in advance there's a good chance it would have been reported in the Worcestershire press, in particular the august *Berrows Journal* (est. 1753), which had always taken a keen interest in the Gents' exploits. But their first article about the tour was published on 31 July 1937, only a few days before the team was due to depart for Berlin.

There is another factor: Middlesex's opposition that day was Worcestershire. The German press reported that Tschammer und Osten and Major Maurice Jewell had spoken before the tour. It was almost certainly at that match on 23 July. As an MCC member, a former captain of Worcestershire, a friend of the chairman of selectors and still heavily involved in the running of the county club, it's also extremely likely the Major was at the same lunch as Tschammer und Osten. Did the subject of a tour to Germany arise then? And did Jewell offer the services of the Gentlemen of Worcestershire, a deal brokered by Plum Warner? There are clues to suggest it was organized in haste: many of the regular Gents players were missing from the final party, and during the tour one

German magazine reported that the Gents had cancelled a number of fixtures to be there, which would not have been necessary had it been arranged a year in advance. It is also possible that an invitation was sent and accepted, the Gents of Worcestershire were the team chosen to tour, but the matter was forgotten until the Reichssportführer's arrival in England, and then an itinerary was hastily put together. Immediately after their meeting, according to the German football magazine *Die Fußball-Woche*, the Major wrote a letter to Berlin (to whom is not known – presumably the Ministry for Sport) declaring his intention to bring a team and listing the names of his players.

The news of the tour broke the day after Tschammer und Osten's lunch at Lord's: Sir Home Seton Charles Montagu Gordon, 12th Baronet Gordon of Embo, Sutherland, mentioned it in his weekly column 'In the Pavilion' in *The Cricketer*, published on 24 July. Despite his grand title, Sir Home Gordon was a roving cricket journalist, instantly recognizable around the county grounds of England by the red carnation he always wore in his buttonhole. He revealed that the Worcester Gents were visiting Berlin on their annual tour and they would arrive in the German capital ten days later. But he didn't disclose the identity or standard of the opposition. Cricket in Germany was a mystery to the English.

3

NICHT KRICKET

THE PROSPECT OF an English team touring Berlin raised a few smiles in the pavilion at Lord's and beyond, where the widespread, stereotypical belief was that Germans were temperamentally unsuited to the greatest of games. But the truth is that cricket and Germany have shared a secret history for more than two centuries. The first detailed, published guide to the game wasn't printed in England but in the Bavarian village of Schnepfental in 1796, as part of a collection of texts on pastimes bearing the snappy title *Games and Exercises for the Relaxation of the Body and the Mind for Young People, Their Instructors, and All Friends of the Innocent Joys of Youth*. The author was a teacher named Johann Christoph Friedrich Gutsmuths who three years earlier had written a book on gymnastics for young people, according to Martin Wilson, the translator of Gutsmuths' treatise on cricket.

In his introduction, Gutsmuths tells us of cricket, 'This game, with which we are now familiar, was brought over from England' without mentioning how it became familiar. In terms of how the sport was 'brought over', Wilson suggests it might have been a series of four matches played at Montbrilliant Palace near Hanover by the Duke of York and invited friends. Three of the matches were won by 45 runs, which would surely have caught the attention of match-fixing investigators these days, and each match was played for a prize of 1,000 guineas (which adds another layer of suspicion). Given how accurate and exhaustive his guide is, Gutsmuths must have played in or watched a match himself. He enjoyed it, too. 'In all seriousness, it is a magnificent game which lends itself to being played (even without money) by young and old; as a game for money (not least when adults cannot play anything else) it is greatly preferable to cards, because here at least the money is laid out with very real benefits to health.'

As endorsements go, 'It's better for you than cards' is hardly ringing. But Gutsmuths was so enchanted by cricket that he felt it didn't require lavish praise. 'There is no need to give cricket a lengthy eulogy; it speaks for itself because it has almost everything that one could ask from an active game. It is splendid open-air exercise, which affords many pleasures, exercises the upper and lower limbs through running, throwing and hitting, is an innocent pastime, and may be played well and enjoyably without financial gain, as actively or gently, as you wish. At the same time, it exercises the intellectual capacities in many ways, and demands a good deal of attention.' To which one can only add: *Das Amen*.

Despite his commendation, Gutsmuths' countrymen remained impervious to cricket's charms. Apart from the occasional match involving exiled Englishmen there is little evidence of anyone in Germany playing cricket anywhere for several decades after his book was published. Germany played France in an unofficial Test in Hamburg in 1865, but both teams were filled with English amateurs. As that century drew to its end the game gained a foothold in Berlin, where English students were fond of playing at Tempelhof, a park once owned by the Knights Templar (hence its name) which became the site of the city's first airport in 1923, but the locals remained unimpressed: in *Cricket Highways and Byways*, F. S.

Ashley-Cooper describes promenading Germans stopping to watch games of cricket 'looking on in stolid silence', unable to fathom its mysteries. Ashley-Cooper also recounts a story of a group of passers-by who were intrigued enough to take a closer look until one of them was hit by the ball.

Nonetheless, by the late 1880s a small group of Berliners had started playing the game. Most belonged to newly established football clubs such as Germania, Preussen and Britannia and had taken up cricket as a way of keeping in shape during the summer off-season. But any hope it might prosper in the slipstream of football's success proved far-fetched. Football was still very much an underground sport in Germany in the late nineteenth century. According to Ulrich Hesse-Lichtenberger in his history of German football, many Germans disliked the game and referred to it as 'the English disease'. In 1898 a gymnast and teacher named Karl Planck wrote with Prussian haughtiness, 'We permit ourselves to regard this anal English sport as not just nasty but absurd, ugly and perverted.'

As football increased in popularity reactionary voices like Planck's started to fade. But cricket remained a minority pastime, almost exclusively confined to Berlin, where the scene was still dominated by English expatriates. Over time, however, it began to seduce some of the locals and gained enough credibility to attract some typically Germanic orderliness. The Deutsche Fussball und Cricket Bund* was founded in Berlin in 1892; then the German authorities

---

* The Germans, confusingly, sometimes refer to cricket as 'Kricket' and other times as 'cricket'. Here, for the title of the organization, they used the English spelling.

decided to classify various sports and activities. Cricket
received the highest ranking: *Schlagball erste klasse*. The
Germans were also keen to stamp their own identity on the
game and developed their own cricketing lexicon: a batsman
became *Schlagmann*, a bowler became *Ballman*, the wicket
was known as *Tor*, and the umpire was the *Schiedsrichter*.
Both teams were required to line up a quarter of an hour
before the match for inspection. The rules were also open to
Teutonic interpretation, as a Dutch touring team discovered.
In one encounter the home team's umpire started giving
batsmen out whenever the ball hit their leg, regardless of
whether it was in line or would have gone on to hit the wicket.
Eventually one of the Dutch players' patience snapped and he
asked why the umpire insisted on putting his finger up so
regularly. 'That is the normal custom in Germany,' he was
told. To which he replied, 'Suppose we play according to the
rules of the MCC and not of the German Emperor!'

The sport continued to develop as the nineteenth century
gave way to the twentieth. The Berlin League was created.
Matches were played on football grounds during the two
months they weren't in use, and at its height the league
boasted fourteen teams, while more touring sides arrived
from the Netherlands and Denmark to play matches against
the stronger clubs such as Victoria and Preussen. Then, in
1911, Leicester Cricket Club became the first ever English
team to visit Germany, led by the Reverend Frank Seaward
Beddow, a pastor and peace activist. Beddow and his team
felt a zeal to spread the good word about cricket. Though,
according to James Coldham, 'their desire to educate the
Germans in the finer points of the game was difficult to
fulfil'. The Berlin batsmen 'seemed to have no definite idea

of playing a straight bat'. They were also rather fond of two-hour lunch breaks which involved lengthy speeches.

The Leicester team won all four matches comfortably, including a final match against a Berlin XI comprising the city's best players. A Grand Banquet followed, where the tourists and their guests sang songs and exchanged gifts. The merriment spilled from the clubhouse on to the field and the Rev. Beddow stood to thank his hosts for their hospitality, offering the hope that the game of cricket might improve the character of Germans as it had done for the English. Whether it was grievance at that perceived slight, or the Prussian equivalent of a jobsworth, Beddow's speech was interrupted by a loud voice who informed him that giving a speech in an open space was illegal and he was liable for a fine of twenty marks. Thankfully his German hosts managed to spare their guest's embarrassment when they settled with the police the next morning.

Perhaps encouraged by a visit from a prestigious English club, the cricket authorities managed to gain independence from football and in 1913 founded the Deutsche Cricket Bund. A year later it was dissolved owing to the outbreak of the First World War during which a number of German cricketers were killed or wounded. But rather than wither and die the sport was resurrected immediately after the cessation of hostilities and began again to grow in popularity. The Treaty of Versailles and the arrival of the British Army on the Rhine together with bodies such as the Disarmament Commission meant an influx of Englishmen, many of whom fancied a game of cricket. When the Berlin Cricket League re-formed, their presence swelled the number of players and teams competing, and Englishmen and Germans, so recently divided by a brutal war, now played sport side by side.

The German game reached such a level of popularity that it attracted the attention of *The Times*. In August 1921 its correspondent filed a report of a match between a Prussian XI and a 'picked team from Holland'. 'A series of games had been arranged by the "Society for the Encouragement of Playing Ball", with a view to popularizing cricket [here spelt Kricket], and doubtless some professor will ultimately provide the necessary proof that the game was really of German origin,' he harrumphed (it would have been interesting to note his reaction if he'd learned that a German had written the first printed guide to the game). The rest of the article is in the same sardonic vein. The field of play was a 'football ground quite innocent of the attentions of a mowing machine, hosepipe, or roller, the pitch being a strip of about 28 yards of some kind of matting'. The Prussians scored 44 in their first innings. The Dutch opening batsmen 'after having given an average of two chances per run both got out', and the score had reached 43 when it was 'unfortunately the time for your correspondent to leave'. He had not been impressed by the standard of play: 'the first straight ball that did not rise over the batsman's head usually got his wicket. Or if it did not, there were two chances, for the batsman either hit it into the air or hit him in the neck.' The standard of sportsmanship did please him, though: 'It need only be added that the match was played in the proper spirit of the game, though the phrase "nicht kricket" has not yet been crystallized into the German language.'

The German press also reported the match and by the end of the decade the country's most popular football magazine, *Die Fußball-Woche*, was running weekly reports of league matches. A German journalist based in London, Rudolf Kircher,* wrote three best-selling books about the English and their customs for an eager audience back home, including a rose-tinted chapter about the 'poised silence' of cricket in *Fair Play: The Games of Merrie England*. 'If you ask an Englishman what the typical national sport is, his answer would not be football! The answer would be Cricket . . . [it] is a specific, English ideology, a key to the English soul, a product of the English spirit. The sport wasn't invented or organized by a sports academic. Cricket grew in an organic, popular way just like a folk dance or folk song is created – as a conversation between people living in a village.' For the German Anglophile, cricket embodied all that was good and decent about the English.

In 1930 the sport was sufficiently strong for a German team to be sent on an eventful tour of England, followed by a reciprocal tour to Berlin by Dartford CC in 1931. Cricket in Germany was on the cusp of respectability. Some clubs set up junior teams and the first youth matches in six years were played in 1931. An unnamed amateur poet was moved to commemorate the event in verse in a German sports magazine:

---

* Kircher returned to Berlin in 1930 where he endured an uneasy existence as a journalist under Nazi rule, not least because of his homosexuality. To escape persecution he was sent to Rome, but had to return from there after being threatened with blackmail for his 'perversions'. However, he survived the war and died in Stuttgart in 1954.

Halfway declared dead,
No one asked about
A sport we thought was lost,
Cricket is back!
From a small hidden place
Cricket steps into the light
And is played everywhere,
Our beautiful Cricket!
Yes, Cricket is making a comeback:
We were happy to hear that
Our youth is championing it!
How can anyone doubt it?
What had not been for six years
Has finally happened:
On Sunday the youth were out to play
And won in many ways.
The signal was now given,
Everywhere there is new life!
Straight ahead we go! The road is free!
Our youth is on board!

But when Hitler and the Nazis gained power in 1933, cricket would lurch back into darkness.

So why did the Germans allow a group of gentlemen from the Malverns to play cricket in their capital? The Nazis were no real fans of the English and no real fans of modern sport. As soon as they gained power they legalized sabre-duelling, known as the *Mensur*, where the object was to inflict a scar on your opponent's face. The body was protected by armour but the duellers did not wear masks. If either flinched then the other was allowed a 'free cut'. It became a sign of honour to walk around with a scar. In fact the victor was often the one who ended up with the most obvious and painful wound. Being able to take these cuts without showing pain was more valued than duelling prowess.

As well as reviving ancient pastimes, the Nazis transformed existing sport in Germany. When compared with the systematic persecution of Jews, the murder and torture of dissidents, the destruction and outlawing of any political opposition, the abandonment of democracy, the abolition of free speech and the rapid rearmament that would make a second world war a certainty, the politicization of much of Germany's sporting and recreational life seems trivial. But the Nazification of sport under the swastika was another defeat for all that was humane and tolerant.

In their desire to micro-manage every part of German life and weed out those who were opposed to the regime, Nazi officials were put in charge of clubs, leagues and associations. Sporting clubs became no-go areas for Jews, communists, trade unionists, some churchmen and others who found themselves in opposition to the state. This stifling control served only to drive people away from games in general and cricket in particular. After 1933 the number of teams dwindled from twelve to four: Preussen, BSV 92, Kickers and Amateure.

The upheavals in German society forced many men to the wayside, either through imprisonment, death or quiet resistance. Harald Poelchau, the son of a Protestant clergyman, was among the Berlin squad that toured England in 1930, though he was a batsman of limited talent. He followed his father into the faith and in 1932 took a job at Tegel Prison where a year later he was made chaplain, at the same time as the jail started to fill with the victims of Nazi intolerance and brutality. Poelchau became a confidant and a comfort to thousands of persecuted men and women, often accompanying them to their death on the gallows. He grew to despise the Nazis and their methods. When members of the Resistance were sentenced, Poelchau used his position to pass messages to them from outside: he arrived at work with secret notes and gifts of food from relatives and associates of the condemned stuffed inside the pockets of his loose-fitting coat and hidden in the lining of his attaché case.

There were others like Poelchau whose work meant they had no time for cricket. There may have been some who were imprisoned for their beliefs. Under the Nazis, far from being *Schlagball erste klasse*, cricket was now barely tolerated. Much of Hitler's appeal was to a sense of nationhood and destiny. Presumably those cricketers who became card-carrying members of the Nationalsozialistische Deutsche Arbeiterpartei (NSDAP), among the millions of people who joined in the first heady months of Hitler's Chancellorship, no longer wished to play a game which their leaders deemed effeminate and un-Germanic.

For cricket and other less celebrated sports in Germany under Hitler's regime the turning point was the infamous 1936 Olympics. Before he rose to power, Hitler viewed the Games as 'an invention of Jews and Freemasons' that 'could not possibly be put on in a Reich ruled by National Socialists', as Guy Walters put it in his superb book *Berlin Games*. But after becoming Chancellor, and emboldened by Joseph Goebbels, his Minister of Propaganda and Public Enlightenment, Hitler was persuaded that hosting the Games would be of immense benefit. First, it would promote health and fitness among German youth, which was of huge importance to the Nazis. Secondly, and perhaps more crucially, it would act as an exhibition of German strength and vigour. 'Sport would be turned into a vehicle of nationalist politics and propaganda as never before,' wrote historian and Hitler biographer Ian Kershaw. 'Nazi aesthetics of power would never have a wider audience. With the eyes of the world on Berlin, it was an opportunity not to be missed to present the new Germany's best face to its hundreds of thousands of visitors from across the globe.'

The abiding myth of the Berlin Olympics is that Jesse Owens' four gold medals undermined the Nazi belief in Aryan superiority and enraged Hitler. The reality is more complex. Far from believing them to be a failure, the regime regarded the Games as a roaring success. The Germans had won significantly more medals than any other nation – an outcome which the National Socialists believed proved conclusively they were the strongest sporting nation on the planet.

To prevent any guests seeing the 'dark side' of the regime, for that summer they suppressed the virulent anti-Semitism which defined it. They took down signs forbidding Jews from entering restaurants and public buildings, Jewish German athletes were allowed to train and compete in the Games, and public violence towards Jews – a feature of the regime in its early years – was prohibited. The Nazis became unusually hospitable towards their guests. Seven thousand prostitutes who had been banned from plying their trade were allowed back on the streets to cater to the needs of foreign visitors. Some gay bars were allowed to re-open, and the Gestapo were even ordered to go easy on any non-German homosexuals caught *in flagrante*. With few exceptions, foreign visitors left Berlin with a favourable opinion of the city, Germany and its rulers, among them Jesse Owens.* Instead of returning to the USA to lecture about the evils of Nazism and his role in embarrassing Hitler, he campaigned for Republican candidate Alf Landon against the incumbent Franklin D. Roosevelt in the 1936 election, during which he referred to Hitler as a 'man of dignity' and derided Roosevelt as a socialist. Landon was defeated in a landslide.

A troop of aristocratic English MPs and lords had also made the journey to Berlin, a number of whom admired Hitler for presiding over an economic 'miracle'. He'd also earned their respect for the way he had crushed the communist threat – a real concern for the moneyed classes of England. Some loathed the idea of another war after the horrific experiences of 1914–18 and would do anything to avoid it, even if it meant caving in to his growing territorial demands. British public morale was low in 1936. The year had started inauspiciously with the death of George V and closed with the crisis over the abdication of Edward VIII. Between those two seismic events there was growing concern over mass unemployment which culminated in the Jarrow March. Meanwhile, in the

---

* The irony was that Owens suffered a far greater degree of racism back in the USA. That year, 1936, was an election year, and one of the reasons he did not give his support to President Roosevelt was that he felt 'snubbed' by the latter for not sending him a congratulatory telegram after his Olympic success. Roosevelt did not want to risk white votes in the Deep South by being seen to kowtow to a black man.

distance, was the gathering storm of war, for which Britain wasn't prepared. Given the choice of appeasing a repugnant regime or suffering another crushing conflict, many were willing to hold their noses and settle for the former.

One prominent group on an Olympic junket was the Anglo-German Fellowship, a shadowy group of aristocrats, businessmen and politicians whose aim was to lobby the British government for closer links with Nazi Germany. Hitler entertained them at a function at the Chancellery. Many returned gushing about their experiences – David Lloyd George referred to Hitler as the 'greatest German of the age'. Thankfully, their word had little effect. Despite being financed by the National Socialists in Germany, Oswald Mosley's fascist party still remained on the fringes of the mainstream and would soon implode.

Few of those upper-class men and women who voiced their admiration for Hitler and his policies moved in English cricket circles. The most famous exception was C. B. Fry, without doubt the most colourful man to have played cricket for England, or any other club, county or nation for that matter. Fry played twenty-six Test matches for his country, equalled the long jump world record, played full-back for England at football and the Barbarians at rugby union, and was also something of an acrobat: his party piece was to leap from the floor, turn in the air and land on a mantelpiece before bowing to his audience. Off the sporting field, and away from the fireplace, he stood as a Liberal candidate for Brighton, gained the rank of Captain in the Royal Naval Reserve, wrote several cricket books, commentated on the radio, and once claimed he had been approached to be King of Albania.

In 1934, Fry, by now losing his mental faculties, had travelled to Germany where he met Hitler and Joachim von Ribbentrop, the Special Commissioner for Disarmament who would later become ambassador to Great Britain. At a dinner with the Anglophile von Ribbentrop, Fry encouraged his host to improve Anglo-German relations by investing money in training a cricket eleven that might be able to compete with England. Von Ribbentrop shrugged off the suggestion: cricket was too complicated a game for Germans, he argued, adhering to the English stereotype. Fry disagreed and told him that given time they might produce a 'blonde W. G. Grace', which creates a pretty ghastly image. Given their natural athleticism and sporting prowess, Fry was convinced it would take only a few weeks for the Germans to produce a team of fielders with the necessary skills, even if producing quality batsmen and bowlers might take longer. Von Ribbentrop remained unconvinced.

When Fry met Hitler, cricket was not a subject for discussion. Von Ribbentrop acted as translator – an onerous task, as both Fry and Hitler were renowned for being fond of the sound of their own voices. Indeed after the war the famous cricket writer Neville Cardus rued the fact that Fry did not speak German; had he been able to, the war might have been avoided as 'Hitler might have died of a fit trying to get a word in'.

Even though the sport didn't come up in that meeting, there is a good chance that in the afterglow of the Berlin Olympics, when he was based in England, von Ribbentrop remembered his dinner conversation with Fry and his exhortations for Germany to take a greater interest in cricket. The regime was keen to cash in on the propaganda success of the Games by continuing to win and influence foreign friends. So when Tschammer und Osten issued the tour invitation and the Gentlemen of Worcestershire accepted, the German Embassy in Berlin wasted no time in providing the Gents with the papers they would need to move around freely and securely, unlike most other foreigners travelling in and out of Berlin. Indeed they would be treated like special envoys.

4

TEUTONIC PHLEGM
AND FLAIR

Had Felix Menzel been born an Englishman there might now be a blue plaque outside the house where he once lived, honouring his existence. If not, his achievements would have been widely recorded. At the very least someone would now know that he had lived. As it is, Felix Menzel is an enigma, ignored and forgotten, a man who fell through a crack in time. For the most part the Gentlemen of Worcestershire were the type of men whose worldly deeds were periodically documented and stored by statisticians, genealogists, historians and college archivists; their German opposition were, according to James Coldham, 'drawn from the ranks of civil servants, lawyers, small shop-keepers, students, academics and Protestant pastors' and left little trace. Such footprints as they did leave were washed away by the furious storm of war. No one I contacted in Berlin or German cricket circles had heard of Felix Menzel, or Fips as he was more commonly known.

His birthdate, like much of his biography, is uncertain. He was born in either 1890 or 1891. He made his debut for Preussen in 1908 in his late teens and was part of the side that played against the touring Leicester CC in 1911. In that match he made an impression by launching a six into a nearby park of such distance that it came to be known as the biggest hit by a German national and briefly became the Teutonic equivalent of the six struck by Albert Trott in 1899, which cleared the pavilion at Lord's. More than a century on, Trott's 'sixer' remains part of cricket legend. Felix's strike was quickly forgotten.

The paucity of information about German cricket means that little else is known of Felix Menzel's career other than that he was primarily a seamer who, like many bowlers, liked to attack rather than defend when his turn came to bat. He fought in and survived the First World War – there is a suggestion he was wounded – and then returned to Berlin where he resumed his cricket. James Coldham suggests he worked as a jewellery dealer. In Berlin address books of the time, now available online, there are two Felix Menzels who fit his description. One was a merchant in Siemensstadt, a suburb of Berlin built to serve the electronics factory, though most people who lived there worked at or had some connection with Siemens. The second Felix lived in Prenzlauer Berg district, at Strassburger Strasse 32. His occupation is given as *Vergolder*, which translates as a gilder. His address was a typical Berlin *Mietskaserne*, a large tenement that housed sixty families – outwardly unassuming and unspectacular, much like Felix himself.

After the war he became one of the most respected cricketers in Berlin. In 1930 he was selected for the United Berlin team, which was the first German team to tour England. The Agricultural and General Engineers had arranged the visit in conjunction with the Federation of British Industries in Berlin, presumably to strengthen trade links, but as two expat Englishmen who worked for the FBI, George Henderson and Francis Jordan, were also well-known members of the Berlin cricket scene, and Henderson was part of the touring party, it may just have been an excuse for an expenses-paid jolly. The events of 1914–18 were still fresh in the minds of many and the tour was not free of controversy. If 1930 had not been an Ashes summer, and if a young Don Bradman had not scored 974 runs in five Tests at an average of 139.14, the Berliners might have attracted more publicity. That said, their brief stay wasn't short of press interest – though not for what happened on the field.

Felix's younger brother Guido, a robust all-rounder, captained the side. There were several others who would face the Gents seven years later, such as Alfred Ladwig, who conforms to the stereotype of insane wicketkeepers who play through the sort of pain that has other cricketers wailing for a physio. As a young man Ladwig had been a talented sportsman: a long-distance runner and a pacy half-back for BFC Preussen as well as an all-rounder on the cricket pitch. But he suffered severe wounds to his feet and legs in the First World War. Most men would have given up sport as a result, but Ladwig converted himself into a goalkeeper and wicketkeeper and wore a pair of specially adapted boots to cope with his injuries. A photo from the 1930 tour shows him walking on to the field in what appear to be a pair of black orthopaedic shoes.

The team arrived in London on the evening of 1 August after travelling third class all the way. Two players made a makeshift bed from 'a plank of wood, fastened with a piece of string from the luggage-rack netting, and served as a support for the head and arms', and food consisted of sardines, rollmops and pickled cucumber. The next morning they travelled to The Oval to watch Surrey play Nottinghamshire. It's easy to imagine the excitement of the German players at the prospect of visiting one of the most famous grounds in the world to watch some of the game's greatest names:

George Gunn, Bill Voce and a young Harold Larwood for Notts; Jack Hobbs, Percy Fender and Alf Gover for Surrey. They paid their own admission, but the start was delayed by rain. The public stands were uncovered, but when they tried to take shelter in the main stand under the pavilion they were refused entry, even though there were rows of empty seats. It was customary for touring sides to be allowed access to the pavilion. George Henderson tried to explain this to a steward but when his request was passed upstairs to the Surrey secretary, Richard Palairet, the answer was still no. The Germans had no choice but to sit in the open stands in the rain.

News of the incident reached the press. The *Daily Mail* went in strongest: 'German Tourists' Cold Welcome' was their headline on Monday, 4 August, 'Surrey Refuse Them Seats'. The report implied the Berliners had been turned away because of their nationality. Other newspapers took a similar tone: whatever a man might think of the Germans, this was cricket, by God, and in cricket a custom was there to be honoured, not broken. 'Such a gesture at the Mecca of English cricket and the shrine of the great Jack Hobbs is an affront alike to English hospitality and English cricket,' thundered the *Exeter and Plymouth Gazette*. 'It has caused intense indignation and the Prince of Wales, who is ground landlord of The Oval, might well reconsider his policy of letting the enclosure at a peppercorn rent. The MCC is pretty autocratic, but at least it has some glimmering of sporting manners.'

The brouhaha brought a swift response from Surrey. In a letter to George Henderson, released to the press, Palairet, a wintry-looking man, decided to shoot the messenger.

He explained that when he had been asked whether any privileges had been granted to the German eleven, he thought it was a reference to the forthcoming Test match. 'If I had realised that all members of the team were present and were asking for admission for the day, I should at once have arranged for their admission, this being the usual practice at the Oval.' He passed on his sincere apologies for the 'quite unintentional slight'. Palairet would move on to creating bigger international controversies: he was joint manager, with Plum Warner, of the England team on the Bodyline tour in 1932/33.

After a day sightseeing in London, where they attended Sunday services at Westminster Abbey and St Paul's Cathedral, the team travelled to Dartford for the first match of the tour. It was 4 August, the date on which Great Britain had declared war on Germany in 1914 – or the date when 'a sterner struggle' began, according to the *Kentish Times*. 'Is it not a happy augury that the first cricket match between Germans and Englishmen should take place on that particular date, and here at Dartford, where many German wounds were healed at the Lower Southern Hospital?' A woman aptly named Rosemary Britain disagreed. 'I understand that August 4th, 1914 is to be commemorated in Dartford next Monday by giving a civil welcome to a German cricket team,' she wrote in a letter to the editor. 'What a delightful way of remembering. Might I suggest as an addition that the name of the town be changed to "Dhartfordt" and that at least some of the townsmen who were prisoners-of-war in Germany for years should perform the re-christening ceremony?' Her letter kicked off a row. Mr A. Spencer Boyse wrote to ask if Ms Britain was 'aware that peace has been made with

Germany? Or does she fail to realise that peace – real peace – means more than the cessation of active hostilities?' Another correspondent called her a 'chauvinist'. Bringing an end to the discussion, the editor, presumably delighted that his letters page was livelier than usual, said tactfully that he was looking forward to the match.

Oblivious to the tumult at the parish pump, the United Berlin team arrived at Dartford CC. They were staggered to find that five thousand spectators had turned up to watch. As the correspondent from *Die Fußball-Woche* (or *FuWo* as it is commonly known) put it, 'This was naturally a shock, as in Berlin one needs a magnifying glass to see any spectators, and the large number put the Berliners in a state of high excitement.'

The unseasonably wet August weather had held off and the team were granted thirty minutes' practice before play. This session marked the first time any of the squad had ever played on a turf wicket, and it soon became apparent they might struggle. All their matches were played on matting, which would be punctured and torn by spikes, so none of the team wore cricket boots. The earlier morning rain had made the surface so greasy that the Germans found it difficult to keep their footing in their tennis shoes.

Before the toss, both teams posed for a group shot with various local dignitaries who had come to watch. Guido Menzel handed a silk pennant bearing the arms of Berlin to his opposite number, C. M. Bryant, and then won the toss and decided to bowl, perhaps fearful that his inexperienced side would be skittled on a green English wicket. As the Germans took the field at 11.30, they were accompanied by the chairman of Dartford Urban District Council who had the honour of bowling the first delivery on this significant occasion. Rather than hit the ball back gently, as is customary, the Dartford batsman Peter Dennis struck it for six and there was a short delay while the fielders retrieved the ball. Perhaps he was smarting from having an application for planning permission refused.

Once play began, Felix Menzel became the first German to take a wicket in England when he bowled E. Lambkin with an inswinger that clipped the leg stump. Dartford went on to score 172, with all-rounder Franz Hustan taking three wickets, including two in successive balls. The *Kentish Times* was impressed with the Berliners' out-cricket. 'Bowling and fielding, the visitors had done very creditably in their first match. Though the placing of the field seemed to indicate some lack of experience, the individual work of the men was keen and good. Their enthusiasm was beyond question and all their efforts and successes were warmly and apprecia-tively applauded.'

The lunch break was extended for speeches during which Councillor White, whose ceremonial opening ball had been smashed out of the park, laid the blueprint for the Basil Fawlty School of not mentioning the war. He reminded the home team they were playing not only for the 'honour of their town, but Kent and the honour of England'. 'His opinion was that on the ground of sport the two great German and British nations would have much in common and it was his sincere hope that the years to come would see these two countries working side-by-side for the betterment of humanity generally,' the *Kentish Times* reported.

When Berlin went out to bat it was soon clear their strength was in the field and not at the crease. The first seven batsmen, Felix and Guido Menzel among them, mustered a meagre twenty-six runs and it was left to the tail to add some respectability. Ample resistance, in every sense, came from the Falstaffian figure of Arthur Schmidt who scored 22 and 'created great amusement by the disdainful manner in which he treated balls not quite to his liking, allowing them to hit his portly person in the most unconcerned way'. He also managed to strike a mighty six 'which pleased the spectators almost as much as it did him'. The tourists were eventually bowled out for 113, a defeat of 59 runs. The Germans asked for a second innings to give them more practice on turf wickets. If it was meant to boost their confidence, it was a failure: by the time the light was gone and stumps were drawn, they had lost nine wickets for forty runs. There was time for a few post-match pints of beer in the bar before they caught the 9.35 back to London.

Their next match, against the Civil Service Crusaders at Chiswick, ended in a rain-affected yet creditable draw. Felix Menzel was the hero with his nagging medium pace, taking four wickets; when play ended Berlin were just forty-one runs short of their target with four wickets remaining. 'Even with the Crusaders, who, as is well known, only have high-level civil servants as members, an atmosphere of brotherly friendship reigned,' ran the report in *FuWo*. 'The first thing the Crusaders' Captain did once the match was over was arm himself with several bottles of beer and share them out among his opponents.'

As a result of their run-in with cricket officialdom the Germans were the toast of the town and received so many invitations they had to turn some down. An unnamed 'rich Indian' gentleman offered to pay them to tour India, which they declined. But they did accept a less exotic offer. 'The fairer sex played their part as well, and a lady of English society invited our teammates to tea and dancing in the Savoy, out of gratitude at the wonderful time she had spent in Germany,' noted *FuWo* in a later summary of the tour.

The evening's entertainment wasn't the only culture shock. On-field behaviour in England was very different to what they knew back in Berlin. The umpires wore 'white coats like our surgeons' and their decision was to be respected at all times, which obviously wasn't the case in Germany. 'There is absolutely no challenging the umpire's decision, and even if he's wrong – "Tough luck," says the Briton. He says the same thing when a player makes a mistake, even when it happens to him. In such cases in Germany one sees gloomy faces, and sometimes rather unharmonious shouts can be heard in the roar of the spectators. Because of this, cricket is the most genteel sport the islanders know. A cricketer will always be a gentleman on the field, whatever social class he belongs to. Indeed, "cricket" has already become an adjective, meaning the same as "gentlemanlike".'

Back on the field, the Berliners' third opponents were Parkdale in a twelve-a-side match. Their frail batting was exposed again: they were dismissed for a paltry 30 on a wet, green wicket. The hosts found the conditions less tricky and after racking up 219 they bowled the Germans out for 75 to complete a chastening defeat by an innings and 114 runs. That second innings could have been worse had Felix Menzel and Gerhard Thamer not offered some resistance after United Berlin lost six wickets for eight runs. According to the correspondent of the *Woodford Times*, Felix and Thamer were the only Berlin batsmen who were capable of getting forward to the probing Parkdale bowling, unlike their teammates who were more inclined to play off the back foot and were bowled or judged lbw.

The final match of the tour was at Kempston, Bedford, against a team representing J. & F. Howard Ltd, an engineering company. Their eleven included, rather unfairly, Denys Morkel, a South African Test player and a distant relation of the current South African Test bowler Morne Morkel. He had toured England the year before with South Africa and his right-arm fast bowling was unsurprisingly considered the best in the tourists' attack. The prospect of him bowling at full pace at a group of men some of whom were approaching what the correspondent of the *Bedfordshire Standard* politely described as 'the veteran stage' on a wet pitch in only their fourth game on turf was a terrifying one. The Berliners must have sighed with relief when Howard's batted first, though Morkel was no mug with the bat either. He opened, and the home side reached fifty without loss after just half an hour's play. Morkel was eventually out for 65 with the score on 90, and his dismissal caused a collapse. Howard's were all out for 156. The local correspondent was appreciative of the Germans' efforts in the field, citing their 'passionate concentration' as well as their amiable nature. 'Very pleasant, sociable fellows they seemed, most of them with a useful working knowledge of English, and one in particular with whom it was possible to carry on quite an animated conversation on sport in general. This was W. Kirloskar, keen-eyed and sun-tanned, the best all-rounder in the team, who took five Howard's wickets for 44. There was little of traditional Teutonic phlegm about this young gentleman, whose vivacity suggested rather the Latin type.' Kirloskar was in fact an Indian from Bombay who had spent two years studying in Berlin.

The United Berlin reply began after tea at 5.30. Morkel bowled extremely fast and the second ball of his second over 'shattered' Gustav Parnemann's stumps. Felix Menzel, perhaps mindful of the pace at one end, was out to a loose shot at the other for a duck, caught brilliantly by Morkel, who went on to complete a satisfying all-round game by taking 5 for 41. The only man to resist was the ageing, diminutive Alfred Ladwig in his orthopaedic boots who refused to take a backwards step to Morkel's searing pace. He was struck on the body several times by the South African's 'fast rising balls but pluckily carried on' and was there at the end, on 20 not out, when the last wicket fell with the score on 83.

The Sports Notes section of the local paper criticized the Germans' approach, contrasting the 'fine, careless rapture which is associated with most English teams in friendly matches' with the limited range of strokes the Berlin batsmen unveiled. 'The drive seemed unknown to them, and for the most part they seemed content to play defensively.' The correspondent failed to note that when you have a nasty fast South African Test player steaming in, a man capable of splattering both your stumps and body, it's not easy for batsmen of any standard to lunge forward on to the front foot.

On their off days the German players were invited to attend matches at Old Trafford and Lord's. In Manchester, rain washed out the entire day's play, as it did at the home of cricket, though they were allowed in the pavilion and the Long Room and had lunch with Sir Kynaston Studd, the MCC's president. They marvelled at the old ground's grandeur and unique atmosphere – and the cost of membership, which a newspaper reporter travelling with them calculated incorrectly to be 4,000 marks (that worked out at £196, when in fact a standard membership was no more than £3 a year).

To end things on a gracious note, the Germans were invited back to The Oval on 12 August to spend the last day of their tour watching the second day of the match between Surrey and Middlesex. This time they were not just allowed in the pavilion, they were also treated to lunch by Surrey president H. D. G. Leveson-Gower, a former Test batsman known universally as 'Shrimp' because of his short stature. As an added treat during the lunch break the Germans were allowed to inspect the wicket for the forthcoming Test match against the Australians. According to *The Times*, 'Martin, the head groundsman, attended to explain the mysteries of its preparation, so far as they may be explained to the general. They were also introduced to Hobbs and did obeisance with charming propriety.'

Meeting Jack Hobbs must have been a thrilling experience for Felix Menzel. He took great interest in English cricket and would have been well aware of The Master's name and achievements. In 1930 Hobbs was forty-eight and deep into the twilight of his career. The wicket Felix and his teammates were studying would be the stage of his final Test match four days later; he'd score 47 and 9 in an innings defeat to Bill Woodfull's side. (It would be far more to the liking of Bradman, who would strike an ultimately match-winning 232 that gave Australia a 2–1 series victory.) Hobbs was a modest man, entirely without affectation, and it's certain he would have answered the Germans' questions patiently and offered some words of encouragement. Glancing around the ground at the vast crowd gathered beneath the famous gasholder and at the seats in the old pavilion packed to bursting, after inspecting a Test match wicket followed by the pleasure of meeting and listening to the finest batsman the world had seen, Felix Menzel began to dream. What if one day a German side could play here in front of a crowd like this? What if they could pit their skills against a genius like Hobbs?

Once their audience with The Master was over, the Germans retired to the comfort of the pavilion to watch Surrey take full advantage of an old-fashioned English 'sticky dog' created by overnight rain. Middlesex lost twenty wickets in the day and were defeated by an innings and 171 runs. And so ended the first ever tour to England by a German cricket team.

The German cricketers were photographed at various stages of the tour: in the stands at The Oval by the *Daily Mirror* (who had the picture but failed to get the story of their being refused entry to the pavilion); a group shot at Dartford with the opposition and local councillors eager to get in on the act; and the two teams before the match against the Howard's XI at Kempston. The second of these photos names everyone. The Germans are all wearing crisp blue blazers emblazoned with badges depicting a red bear – an ancient symbol of Berlin. In the midday sun the peaks of their white caps cast shadows across their faces. Felix Menzel is standing in the middle of the back row. The shot is too small to make out too many details but he looks quite broad. He's unsmiling, but then so is everyone. Sitting in front of him, more in the light, squinting into the sun, is his brother Guido. It is easier to find them in the Howard's picture, where they are standing and sitting with the same serious faces, in the same rigid poses. The images give no hint about the character of these men. The original of the photo taken at The Oval, with the team in civvies rather than whites and blazers, has been lost and the copy is too indistinct to tell who is who. It seemed appropriate, as if Felix Menzel was never quite in sight, always just out of reach.

The following summer the Berliners were a more difficult proposition on home soil. The visitors were Dartford, who had beaten them so soundly in their first match of the 1930 tour. This time the Berlin team managed to win two of the four matches thanks to the bowling of Arthur Schmidt, who took 32 wickets at 5.43 each, and Felix Menzel, who took 24 at 6.04 apiece, even though they only played three matches. The Germans were so excited at the prospect of winning the second match (they'd only narrowly lost the first) that they played well into the evening to ensure the victory, even though it meant delaying a banquet which had been arranged in honour of the Dartfordians. Despite the competitive nature of the cricket, the spirit between the two teams remained good. On the Englishmen's departure, the Berliners handed them a bunch of red roses with a card reading: 'Take these roses home with you, Flowers alas must perish, But the thoughts which go with them, May you ever cherish.'

There is a photograph of Felix Menzel in *Die Fußball-Woche*. Schmidt is bowling left-arm around the wicket with an enormous belt around his ample waist the size of a cummerbund. In close-up he looks like a dead ringer for Curley Howard of the Three Stooges. He has just released the ball and it is clear from his action, the low front arm in particular, and his line of sight that he bowled looping left-arm lobs. The sort which look easy to hit from the side but are torture to face, especially when the bowler is able to vary his flight and length as Schmidt was able to, and make use of the variable bounce on a soft, thin piece of matting. The ground around the mat is bare, with only a few tufts of grass. It was a far cry from The Oval. At the non-striker's end is a serious-looking man leaning on his bat, its blade showing more black tape than wood – a testament to years of good use. His receding hair is neatly combed and slicked into shape with a high side-parting; he has a round friendly face and his belt is of normal size, though there are the first signs of middle-aged spread around his waist. It is Felix Menzel.

That cricket didn't die when the Nazis gained power is almost entirely down to Felix's devotion and quiet bravery. Hitler and his cronies had intimidated, jailed and killed all prominent opposition. Fascist belief and dogma had infiltrated every part of German society and Nazi control of all aspects of German civil life was absolute and ruthless. National Socialism was a straight path; to divert from it was to risk instant and often brutal punishment. Meanwhile, the Hitler myth, of a predestined, heroic figure leading Germany back to greatness, encouraged people to do all they could to find his favour. The historian Ian Kershaw described this behaviour as 'working towards the Führer': this refers not just to those in the party fighting like cats in a sack to curry favour with their leader, but also, as Kershaw explained, 'ordinary citizens denouncing neighbours to the

Gestapo, often turning personal animosity or resentment to their advantage through political slur, businessmen happy to exploit anti-Jewish legislation to rid themselves of competitors, and the multitude whose daily forms of minor cooperation with the regime took place at the cost of others, were – whatever their motives – indirectly carrying out their Führer's wishes'.

On the sporting field the myth was embodied by gymnastics performed in massed ranks. The idea was to use sport to breed a generation of strong, vigorous athletes. In the introduction to *Sport und Staat*, commissioned by Hans von Tschammer und Osten, Hitler stated his view that the sole purpose of sport and exercise was to create magnificent young physical specimens that could be put to military and industrial use for the good of the German *Volk*. 'In the Third Reich it is not only knowledge which counts, but also strength, and our absolute ideal for the future would be a human being of radiant mind and magnificent body, that people may again find a way to riches through money and property.'

A 'magnificent body' has never been a prerequisite for cricket, thankfully (a 'radiant mind' is rarely seen either). Neither has the game ever been the most efficient path to a well-sculpted physique. Men of girth have always been attracted to cricket, and that's only partly because it's the only sport to offer two good meals a day while freeing time for breakfast and dinner. Many amateur cricketers tend to put on weight during the cricket season rather than lose it thanks to stodgy teas and copious amounts of post-match beer. It didn't keep you fit, it often made you fat, in Nazi eyes it was effeminate, and it was quintessentially English – it is difficult to think of any other sport or pastime less likely to be described as 'working towards the Führer' than playing cricket. Given the rush to conform and please in 1930s Germany, strapping on a pair of pads constituted a small act of rebellion.

That a sport which was barely tolerated by the regime was in 1937 granted a tour by a foreign side is remarkable. The credit for this must go to Felix Menzel. According to James Coldham, whose father knew and played against Menzel and who later corresponded with him, he was a 'wholehearted publicist for the game'. The fact he managed to reach a position where he had the ear of Tschammer und Osten, the most powerful man in German sport and a high-ranking NSDAP official, is astonishing.

It is even more startling when you consider that Felix was not a Nazi. Millions signed up after Hitler gained outright power, often because not being a member was a barrier to advancement in business, or it sowed suspicion that might lead others to denounce someone to the Gestapo. But in the party membership records and registers held at the Bundesarchiv in Berlin there is no evidence of Felix having joined the party.

So how did he reach the stage where he was able to organize cricket tours, was labelled *Cricketwart* in the press ('cricket presence') as well as *Cricketführer* ('cricket leader') and was later permitted to address the international press, something the Nazis would never trust anyone but their own lackeys to do? The Nazification of German sport meant that party officials were in charge at almost every level. The Gauführer in the Gau III Berlin-Brandenburg region where cricket was played was Franz Breithaupt. He had fought in the First World War and been awarded both classes of the Iron Cross. He joined the Nazi party in 1931, and the Sturmabteilung. A year later, perhaps sensing the SA's waning influence on Hitler, he joined the SS, the party's notorious paramilitary corps. He served as a senior member of the staff of Heinrich Himmler, who would become one of the most powerful men in Nazi Germany. Breithaupt eventually became an Obergrüppenführer, the highest paramilitary rank available behind Himmler, the SS Reichsführer. Felix would have had to deal with senior Nazis like Breithaupt on a regular basis. They knew everything about everybody, so Breithaupt must have been aware he wasn't a party member. So again we must ask, how did Felix become so influential?

In the absence of firm biographical evidence we are forced to speculate. Perhaps Felix the *Vergolder* was able or willing to supply senior Nazi figures such as Breithaupt and Tschammer und Osten with items of jewellery or gold at a price that encouraged them to overlook his non-Nazi status, and gave him a platform to promote his love of cricket and even, in the case of the tour by the Gentlemen of Worcestershire, try to raise its profile among Germans. Tschammer und Osten was a man of expensive tastes and it's hard to resist the image of Felix Menzel exploiting the vanity and greed of leading Nazis like him to buy time, space and prestige for the sport he adored. What we do know is that regardless of circumstances Felix was determined to play cricket, and he would go to great lengths to ensure the sport did not die. In fact his eyes were firmly fixed on increasing cricket's popularity.

In the dark days of 1933/34 when the number of Berlin teams began to dwindle, sensing the hostility of the new regime to the game, Felix must have wondered whether that would happen. So the arrival three years later of a prestigious English team with the blessing of his leaders, creating a stream of media interest, was a tribute to his courage and indefatigability.

5

A MAJOR INFLUENCE

IF EVER THERE was a team able to go on an overseas cricket tour at less than a fortnight's notice it was the Gentlemen of Worcestershire. The club's members were either independent men of leisure or so successful in business they could afford a few days off for a game of cricket. They also relished the challenge of playing in less familiar places. In the 1930s they had been made very welcome in the Netherlands, Portugal and Denmark, though at a fairground in Copenhagen they were banned from the coconut shy after proving such dead-eyed shots that they cleaned the stall out of prizes.

Their captain and senior player, Major Maurice Jewell, was the son of the British Vice Consul in the port of Iquique in Chile, where he was born in 1885. This, together with his swarthy complexion, led other members of the family to refer to him as 'The Chilean', though never to his face. The Major, as he was more commonly known, was not a man to suffer fools gladly.

Beyond family life he had one passion: cricket. Although he'd served during the First World War with distinction, he rarely did any work for a living, which enabled him to devote most of his plentiful time to the greatest of all games, first as a player and then as an administrator. But even as he made the transition from field to committee room he continued to play for the Gentlemen of Worcestershire, well into his fifties.

He flourished late as a cricketer. At Marlborough he was

a useful left-arm slow bowler for his house team, and batted low in the order with little success; there was no indication then that he would play at a high level. After leaving school he went to agricultural college rather than university, where he must have worked hard at his cricket because in 1909 he made his first-class debut for Worcestershire alongside his best friend William Taylor, who was making his second appearance. Unlike Taylor, who opened the bowling and claimed his first first-class wicket, Maurice was making up the numbers: he batted at 10 in both innings (making 10 not out and 4) and didn't bowl.

The Major would have to wait another four years for a game of first-class cricket. In the meantime he moved to Surrey where he lived with his widowed mother and several of his siblings. In 1911 he married William Taylor's sister Elsie. She also happened to be a member of the family who owned Royal Brierley Crystal, which meant a rich source of income to support her and her new husband. Maurice had been managing a dairy before the wedding, but by the time he and Elsie tied the knot he had given up work. On his wedding certificate he gives his occupation as 'Gentleman'. He was twenty-six and an independent man of means, and that meant lots of time for cricket.

In the summer of 1913 he played his second game of first-class cricket, albeit for H. K. Foster's XI, a team led by the former captain of Worcestershire. Once more it was against Oxford University and yet again Maurice didn't bowl, though by scoring 24 in the second innings he managed to eclipse his best first-class score. The next summer he played two late-season matches for Sussex in the county championship as a middle-order batsman and part-time bowler. The first was at Eastbourne against Worcestershire, who were captained by his brother-in-law, in which Maurice scored his maiden first-class half century. Also in that team was nineteen-year-old Maurice Tate, who would go on to score more than 21,000 runs and take almost 3,000 wickets in a domestic and international career spanning twenty-five years.

He retained his place for the next match at the county ground at Hove against Yorkshire, which featured giants of the game like Major Booth, Wilfred Rhodes and George Hirst. Maurice did not bowl and batted only once, in Sussex's first innings, where he became the 400th first-class victim of Alonzo Drake, a slow left-arm bowler of great talent who had taken all ten Somerset wickets in an innings earlier in the season. The match petered out into a draw. Maurice would play no more county matches that season, but then neither would anyone else: Britain had declared war on Germany and the season was brought to a premature conclusion. The cricket grounds of England fell silent as the sound of war began to echo around fierier fields.

Maurice Jewell survived the war. His younger brother Dudley did not, killed in 1916 while serving with the Royal Fusiliers. Cricket suffered grievous losses. The Roll of Honour in the 1920 edition of *Wisden* numbered seventy-seven, and was by no means complete. As a result the 1919 season was almost apologetic in nature, as if sport and games were futile in the aftermath of such slaughter. Fearing that fans might have drifted away from the game after a four-year absence, the authorities discussed a range of gimmicks to try and entice them back, including shorter boundaries, penalizing the batting side for playing out maidens and even banning left-handed batsmen. None was put into action, much to the delight of Sydney Pardon, the gloriously named editor of the *Wisden Almanack*, who described the proposals as 'fatuous' and 'foolish'. The only change to post-war county cricket was the reduction in length of matches from three days to two, which resulted in so many draws that it was swiftly abolished for the 1920 season.

The Major once again played irregularly for Sussex, turning out in four matches in 1919 with mixed success. But he revealed his true loyalties by appearing in seven first-class 'friendlies' for Worcestershire, who had not re-entered the county championship. For two of those matches, against Gloucestershire and Warwickshire, he was even made captain, despite the presence in both teams of his brother-in-law and the side's usual captain, William Taylor. In the second of those matches, against their Midland rivals Warwickshire at New Road, Maurice took 7 for 56 in 17.1 overs, which remained the best bowling figures of his career.

Shortly before the war, Maurice and Elsie had moved to a large Georgian house in Upton-on-Severn in the Malvern Hills. The Hill, as the house was known, would be the Jewell family home for more than fifty years, and the Major would become heavily involved in Upton life as a Justice of the Peace, chairman of the town council and the local 'squire'. There are still some elderly Upton residents alive today who remember receiving 6d each Christmas as a gift from the old Major (changed to an orange in times of rationing). He was not showy by any means, but in 1915 he became the first man in Upton to have a telephone (tel. no. Upton 23).

Worcestershire entered the 1920 championship and the qualification rules for county cricket stated that no player was able to play for more than one county. Now firmly ensconced in Worcestershire, it's unsurprising that Maurice chose to play for them, although it could be argued that Worcestershire chose him. While Sussex were blessed with a stock of good cricketers, Worcestershire needed all the help they could muster. There was no squad, merely a collection of cricketers, most of them amateurs who wished to pick and choose the matches they played in. Some of them were quirky characters who only played a match or two. William Shakespeare, a decorated RAF pilot who completed the first pan-European commercial flight, was one. There was also a clergyman called Richard Fowler who played four matches under M. F. S. Jewell in 1920. He took 5 for 33 against Gloucestershire but was told by the umpire it was only his profession that had prevented him from being no-balled.

Unlike other sides, particularly the successful ones like Yorkshire and Surrey, for the first couple of seasons after the war Worcestershire couldn't afford to buttress their team with wizened professionals. The only reliable pro they were able to call on in 1920 was Fred Bowley, who at forty-seven was hardly one for the future, though he still managed to score almost five hundred runs more than anyone else that season. Another regular was Arthur Jewell, Maurice's brother, who scored two championship centuries. Those were to be his last: four years later, aged just thirty-four, Arthur died of an unspecified illness after a long period of poor health.

Worcestershire's record in 1920 under the Major's

captaincy was execrable: played 18, won 1, lost 16, drawn 1 (and that was down to rain). Even though matches were scheduled for three days it was rare for Worcestershire's to last two and when they played away it was commonplace for the players to book into the hotel for one night because they were so rarely there for a second. Only Derbyshire's hopelessness prevented them from finishing bottom of the table. But the season proved so dispiriting and costly – 'no players, no spectators and no cash' according to one history of the club – that there was every chance the county side would cease to exist.

But the Major and a few other stalwarts refused to bow to the inevitable and they were rewarded with a far more successful season the following year, winning five and losing only fifteen. Humphrey Gilbert took 100 wickets while the ageing Bowley was given good support with the bat by Harry Higgins. The Major also proved he was worth his place in the side by scoring more than eight hundred runs. That season also saw the arrival of Fred Root, a gnarled professional seam bowler who had done his time in the leagues of the North, and who would play a major role in Worcestershire's rise to respectability between the wars. After a season and a half of minimal success with conventional seamers, Root developed a new line of attack: sharp inswing bowling with a cordon of five catchers ranged behind square on the leg side, thus making him the pioneer of leg theory which, thanks to Douglas Jardine and some Aussie whingeing, would soon become maligned and outlawed. Needless to say, Fred Root was unimpressed with the brouhaha that followed the Bodyline series: 'It is all very well to subscribe to all the sentimental nonsense that has been written on the subject "for the good of the game". What would the game be without a fast bowler whose main attribute is power to make lethargic batsmen jump around a bit?'

Maurice Jewell was unfortunate not to benefit from Root's rise, at least as skipper. After the 1921 season he stood down in favour of his brother-in-law, though he was still a regular part of the side for the next three seasons. His appearances dwindled in 1924 and 1925, but in 1926 he was once again made captain, at the age of forty-one. He also proved to be the team's best all-rounder, scoring more than a thousand runs in the season and taking twenty-two useful wickets. Root took 99 at 20 apiece, but his county won only three matches and finished bottom of the table.

The Major made a good impression on Root, even though the bowler, as he made clear in his entertaining biography *A Cricket Pro's Lot*, was not always a fan of the amateur cricketer and the 'snobbish' lot who ran the game. In one match at New Road two Glamorgan batsmen collided mid-pitch. One appeared to be seriously hurt, and when the ball was thrown back to Root at the non-striker's end the batsman, Dyson, was still lying in the middle of the pitch. 'Break the wicket, Fred, break the wicket!' Root recalls one 'keen amateur' shouting. Root turned on him angrily: 'If you want to run him out, here's the ball: *you* come and do it.' The amateur recoiled in horror: 'Oh, I'm an amateur, *I* can't do such a thing.' Root allowed the batsman to be helped off, only for him to come back in when the eighth wicket fell and help Glamorgan salvage a draw. At the close, according to Root, 'Major Jewell blamed me very much for not running Dyson out . . .'

Now in his forties, a regular for the Gents, with a garden to tend to at The Hill and various civic duties, that really should have been the end of Maurice Jewell's first-class career. But he continued to play in 1927, and when it became clear his successor Cecil Ponsonby was proving an ineffectual leader he captained once more in 1928 and 1929, though by now he was battling unspecified ill health which prevented him from playing in every match.

His curtain call as captain came in 1930, the tour opener against the visiting Australians led by Bill Woodfull and featuring Stan McCabe, Clarrie Grimmett and the young Donald Bradman. At second slip the Major was in prime position to be one of the first Englishmen to witness Bradman's genius close up as he scored 236 in less than five hours. The Australians racked up 492 en route to a victory by an innings and 165 runs. Like an old actor reluctant to leave the stage, that still wasn't the end for the Major. He played one more county championship match the following summer, fittingly against the county for whom he had made his debut, Sussex. Two years later he played against Oxford University and then against the touring West Indies. In that last match he scored 3 and 16 and was run out in both innings – a testament to the passing years – before finally leaving the first-class stage for good.

According to *Wisden*, without the Major's dedicated service there is no way the county would have survived the troubled years between the wars:

Those whose memories start in 1946 or later have no conception how much some counties at the bottom of the championship before 1914 and between the wars owed to certain amateurs, often only moderate players who could never have kept a place in a good county side, but who year after year gave up their summer to keeping their county going, captaining it themselves and some-how collecting an eleven for each match, being rewarded at the end with perhaps two or three wins, perhaps less. It was due largely to the devoted labours of such as these that no first-class county ever had to pack up, though some in those days came pretty near it. In this category Jewell stood high.

It is no slur on the Major's cricketing ability to say that his greatest service to Worcestershire came off the pitch rather than on it. Elsie was a talented musician, capable of playing the piano by ear. Together they had four daughters, whom the Major turned into his own musical troupe to entertain guests at The Hill (Young Maurice, their only son, tried to escape these performances by hiding under the piano or in a wardrobe upstairs). Plum Warner gave a vivid description of being entertained by the talents of the Jewell sisters Rosalind, Sonia, Mavis, Renee and Joy. 'I stayed at the Jewells, and their charming and versatile daughters delighted us in the evening with their singing and dancing. During the winter, under the coaching of the Maestro, their father, these "polished daughters of the temple" used to raise considerable sums of money for local charities.'

One of those charities was Worcestershire CCC. The Major was a tireless fundraiser. He formed a concert party which toured the county in the off-season to raise money to pay professionals and improve the club's grounds and facilities. He also organized Grand Bazaars lasting two or three days. In 1933, when the county was £2,247 in debt, the minutes of that year's committee meeting record the Major offering to arrange and host a Pierrot show in which he and his family would dress up as clowns and mime, simply in an effort to reduce the deficit. His persistence and dedication did more than just keep Worcestershire afloat: by the mid 1930s the county side was competitive enough to challenge for a position in the middle of the table rather than languishing at the bottom.

But merely watching and fundraising was not enough to scratch the Major's cricket itch. He still felt the need to play and compete, and by the mid 1930s he was a regular for the Gents. He became captain, and was able to recruit some of the men who had played with him for the county side, which made them one of the strongest amateur sides in the country and willing tourists to boot.

Plum Warner, writing in *The Cricketer* the day before the 1937 tour party was announced, believed the visit to Berlin would help promote the game 'especially as Herr Hitler had shown an interest in cricket'. Where he got that idea from is anyone's guess. Perhaps a well-lubricated Tschammer und Osten had gilded the lily during his long lunch at Lord's. But two of the three matches were to be regarded, by the Berliners at least, as unofficial 'Tests'. This created enough consternation among the committee rooms and bars of the MCC for Warner to warn the Major that he'd rather they didn't lose, given the simmering diplomatic tensions between London and Berlin. Warner was well aware that Maurice Jewell's team featured several former first-class players. The last thing the MCC wanted was for them to be beaten and hand Hitler and the Nazis a propaganda coup.

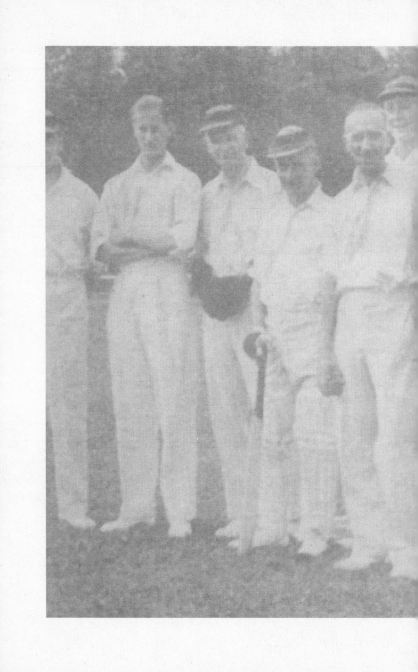

6

THE ROAD TO BERLIN

MAJOR JEWELL'S men were so accustomed to touring abroad they had their own baggage labels printed in the club's colours of green, purple and black and bearing a header that read 'Worcestershire Gentlemen's CC'. The night before they were due to set off, Peter Robinson wrote his name and destination on his in his neatest hand.

The next day was Tuesday, 3 August – a year to the day since Jesse Owens had sprinted into history and the day before the twenty-third anniversary of the outbreak of the First World War. It also marked the third anniversary of Hitler joining the offices of President and Chancellor and becoming supreme Führer of Germany. That morning, Peter Robinson and most of the touring party caught the train from Worcester to Paddington. From there they took the underground to Victoria to meet the rest of the team. On the way they stopped at a Lyons café for lunch, which at a cost of only 1/6 Peter thought 'Marvellous!' If Major Jewell had any time to read his copy of that morning's *Times*, did he note the story by the newspaper's own Berlin correspondent, Norman Ebbutts, about the dawn arrest of a leading figure in the German Confessional Church, who had earned the distrust of Hitler, 'under the law for the protection of State and Party against underhand attacks'? The article mentioned that Pastor Martin Niemoller was still being detained without trial for his criticism of the regime. Niemoller would later become famous for his 'First they came' statement about the apathy of German intellectuals to the regime's growing brutality.*

The boat train departed from Victoria mid afternoon and arrived at Dover Marine ninety-eight minutes later – 'no time' according to Peter Robinson, and in good time to catch the ferry for the crossing to Ostend in Belgium. There had been no scrimping: they were sailing on the diesel-powered *Prince Baudouin* which for a few brief months had been the fastest motor vessel in the world after its launch in 1934, and was still by far the quickest boat on the Dover–Ostend crossing. Three hours later they were at Ostend station to catch the Nord-Express. Even though their journey had run like clockwork, the train's departure had to be delayed a few minutes to give them time to board. They were, after all, first-class passengers and it was not the done thing to leave them behind.

The Nord-Express was 'wizard!' in Peter Robinson's view. Its luxury was matched only by the Orient Express. Such was its romance that *Strangers on a Train*, Alfred Hitchcock's classic psychological thriller, was renamed in French *L'inconnu du Nord-Express* ('The unknown man in the Nord-Express'). The sleeper cars had two berths and Peter Robinson shared with Peter Terry, 'he on top and me

* 'First they came for the communists,
   and I didn't speak out because I wasn't a communist.
   Then they came for the socialists,
   and I didn't speak out because I wasn't a socialist.
   Then they came for the trade unionists,
   and I didn't speak out because I wasn't a trade unionist.
   Then they came for me,
   and there was no one left to speak for me.'

down below'. Maurice Jewell shared with Peter Huntington-Whiteley. (The presence of so many Peters required a method to differentiate between them: Terry was labelled Peter One, Huntington-Whiteley Peter Two, and the baby of the group, Robinson, became Peter Three.)

As the men ate their evening meal in the restaurant car, a far cry from the sardines, rollmops and pickled cucumber the German players had shared on their third-class voyage to England in 1930, the Nord-Express stopped at Brussels and then Liège. Robert Berkeley began to tease the younger players about a fearsome fast bowler who played for the Berlin team.

Captain Berkeley was of landed stock. He had two addresses: Spetchley Park in Worcestershire, which had been in the family since 1606, and Berkeley Castle in Gloucestershire, which his family had owned since 1067. The bed in which Captain Berkeley slept at Berkeley Castle, and which is still occasionally used by his son John, is believed to be the oldest bed in Britain, dating back to at least 1608. Fifteen generations of the family have slept in it.

Berkeley had served with the Westminster Dragoons in Palestine and on the Western Front in the First World War before dedicating his life to three things: his castles, their gardens in particular; hunting (he was Joint Master of Foxhounds for the Berkeley Hunt, the oldest pack in the country and a notable entry in the lexicon of cockney rhyming slang, an abbreviation of which has given us the insult 'berk'); and cricket. His four unsuccessful appearances for the county club between the wars (seven innings, 37 runs, top score 16, with an average of 5.28) belied his elegant, quick-scoring strokeplay.

He was a renowned humorist, and his story of a German bowler of such pace that he once removed the front teeth of a batsman only for him to place the teeth behind the stumps and carry on his innings was entirely fictitious. But the Gents had no clue about what lay in store for them on or off the pitch. All they knew was they had better win for the honour of King, country and the MCC.

As the train rattled through the European night, the men retired to the sleeping carriage and their berths. The August night was warm and Cyril Smith's travelling companion in the bed below – it is not known who it was – opened the window in their cabin. The subsequent draught blew straight on to Smith, who tossed and turned most of the night, bothered by the chill, but didn't close the window. The next morning found him cold, tired and thoroughly fed up.

Unlike their fellow travellers who were required to present their baggage for inspection by customs, the Gents were not disturbed when the train stopped at the border between Belgium and Nazi Germany. The entire side had been granted a 'laissez-passer' by the German Embassy in London which allowed them to pass freely into and out of Germany. According to Robert Berkeley, this 'spared us many inconveniences, such as being woken up at the frontier, in the middle of the night, for the always tedious Customs examination'. The granting of such a document to a group of Englishmen shows how keen the Nazis were for the tour to pass as smoothly as possible, though it's not overly cynical to wonder if they wanted to avoid their guests witnessing an incident that might colour their view of the Third Reich.

Peters One and Three, Terry and Robinson, slept 'jolly well' between the train leaving Brussels and stopping at

Hanover at five a.m. They eventually rose at 7.15 and had a breakfast of coffee, fruit and rolls, then pulled back the curtains for their first view of Nazi Germany. 'The country is quite flat and there are no hedges & plenty of corn' was Robinson's initial, underwhelmed impression.

That Wednesday, 4 August, their train coasted through the Berlin suburbs then alongside the Spree and pulled into Friedrichstrasse, the city's busiest station, at 8.43 a.m. A welcoming party was waiting on the platform. At its head was Hans Wolz of the Deutsche Reichsbund für Leibesübungen, the Nazi Ministry for Sport. Wolz was closely involved with running Berlin football but rugby and cricket also came under his remit. Alongside him were members of the Deutsche-Englische Gesellschaft, the sister organization of the Anglo-German Fellowship. With some justification it was widely perceived as sympathetic to the ideas of Hitler and his party and, as a result, it had come to the notice of the security services, who monitored its activities closely. In London and Berlin its membership was dominated by businessmen and politicians including Geoffrey Dawson, the editor of *The Times*, and the serving Governor of the Bank of England, Montague Norman. It was so right-wing that Guy Burgess and Kim Philby, the British intelligence officers who became double agents and defected to the Soviet Union during the Cold War, were able to deflect any suspicion about their communist sympathies by joining.

The Gents might have anticipated a group of local *Wichtigtuers* (busybodies) to be there to greet them. Less expected were the pack of newsmen and photographers, of whom the most intrepid was a reporter from local football weekly *Das Fußball-Megaphon* who barged his way to the front to put to the visitors the crucial questions. 'Why do you have so much luggage?' he asked, unaware perhaps of the sheer amount of equipment a cricket team requires. 'Oh yes . . . golf,' came the reply from an unnamed Gent. The tourists didn't play a single game of golf on their trip, so someone was displaying a dry sense of humour. The same reporter discovered that Major Jewell was an 'extraordinary bowler' – it is doubtful the Major supplied that description himself – and noted that his son was one of the best players in his county. 'Recently he set a record by achieving 78 runs,' he wrote in his report. Young Maurice was a promising young player but best in the county was pushing it a bit.

From the station the team were taken to the Unter den Linden and their accommodation for the next eight nights. The old boulevard, named after the row of linden or lime trees that lined the central pathway which divided the two carriageways, was now adorned with three towering rows of white columns crowned with gilded swastikas and eagles stretching along its entire length. Many of its buildings were bedecked with red swastika flags. The effect was a stunning, unmissable display of Nazi pageantry and might.

Berlin in 1937 was a city riddled with contradictions. Even though its people had endured an uneasy relationship with Hitler, the city was indisputably the centre of Nazi power. Initially Hitler and his acolytes found Munich, their original power base, more to their taste. In their view, the Berlin of the 1920s had been a licentious, immoral place, a wicked brew of Bolshevism, Judaism and sexual deviance. Neither were Berliners too enamoured of him and his party, to begin with at least. On 31 January 1933, the morning after Hitler gained power, the *Berliner Morgenpost* advised its readers to be vigilant of their new leaders: 'We shall not allow ourselves to be provoked and recommend that everyone who finds the change of Government unedifying does the same.'

There were plenty who found the government 'unedifying', but they were soon outnumbered by those who supported it. Berliners swiftly fell in line with the rest of the country and in the first half of 1933 hundreds of thousands rushed to join the NSDAP; meanwhile, the promise of vigilance from the *Morgenpost* proved to be hollow when the Nazis seized control of the press. Nearly all criticism of the regime was silenced, and those brave enough to speak out about its cruelty were summarily punished. The Nazis reigned by terror but popular support for Hitler in the capital grew, and not simply because the population was bullied into obedience. More by luck than judgement, the increased spending on building projects and rapid rearmament in preparation for war had fuelled a financial boom. Economically, life was far better for Berliners than it had been before 1933. The capital became an industrial powerhouse and unemployment fell dramatically. Any reservations the majority of Berliners had about their dictator were swept away by their appreciation of this rise in living standards. The troubled courtship between Hitler and the Berlin people blossomed into a passionate affair. Countless thousands of people lined the streets for the parades and processions the Nazis were so fond of. In return for their adoration Hitler asked his favoured architect Albert Speer to draw up plans to transform Berlin into the most impressive and powerful city in the world, the capital of the vast German empire he would rule over after the war, rivalling not London or Paris but Alexandria, Babylon, even Ancient Rome.

Despite the antediluvian beliefs of its new overlords, Berlin had retained much of the modern fizz and pizzazz of the Weimar period. Nightlife was still thriving: bars and restaurants were crammed to bursting; cinemas screened Hollywood movies; and even though jazz was officially deprecated as 'Negro' music, many clubs played a version of jazz and swing while the Nazis turned a blind eye. The city had become their playground, a gleaming oasis of modernity in a Nazi culture of provincialism and retarded thought. Like convention-goers in Las Vegas, eager to behave in a manner they never would dream of at home, prominent Nazis flocked to Berlin to cast off their inhibitions and breach the sort of rules they usually enforced with untrammelled brutality in the provinces. Like Vegas, if you were rich and had connections there was no better place to visit than Berlin. Socially at least, the Worcester Gents were certain to have a ball.

Despite official papers allowing them free entry, the Gents were paying their own way in Berlin (as the local press were eager to point out). Given their tastes and collective wealth, it was unlikely they would choose to stay in a backstreet bed and breakfast. But even by their standards the decision to stay at the Hotel Adlon was an extravagant one. In 1937 it was one of the most sumptuous, iconic hotels in the world. During the 1920s it was the bohemian heart of the city, where artists, actors, writers and politicians dined, drank and danced. Louise Brooks, Charlie Chaplin, Josephine Baker, Thomas Mann, Marlene Dietrich and Albert Einstein were regular guests. Because of its popularity with westerners and its reputation for intemperance and licentiousness it was never the hotel of choice for leading Nazis, who preferred the Kaiserhof, located across the road from the Propaganda Ministry and next to the Reich Chancellery on Wilhelmplatz. But the absence of senior members of the NSDAP made the hotel an even more attractive proposition for international journalists and the diplomats who were their main sources, and throughout the day its marble lobby and bars hummed with well-lubricated gossip.

That August morning the bar was humming with weary but thirsty Englishmen as the newly arrived cricket team wasted no time in sampling some German beer. Peter Robinson took to it immediately, even if it was only 9.30 a.m. 'The beer is far nicer here than in England,' he wrote on Adlon-headed notepaper once he had checked into his room, begging the question how much English ale a sixteen-year-old public schoolboy had managed to consume. The beer was not the only thing he found captivating: 'As for the Adlon Hotel, well, it's just a dream! [Peter] Terry and I are in adjoining rooms and share a bathroom, which has an immense bath, a shower, a WC, a footbath, and heated towel rails!' The footbath was actually a bidet, but what was a teenage boy to know of such contraptions? He had already used the bath to slough away the grime of the journey and had found time to buy evening socks, sock suspenders, cufflinks and studs ('all at sale price' he reassured his mother).

The view from Robinson's bedroom window was one of

the most famous in Europe. He was able to gaze across the grandest square in the city, Pariser Platz, to the Brandenburg Gate, the neoclassical triumphal arch which was the capital's most famous landmark. To the north, rising above the skyline, was the dome of the Reichstag, restored to full glory after the fire that had destroyed it four years earlier and given Hitler the excuse to purge the city of his opponents. In the distance were the tall trees of the Tiergarten, the 'Garden of Beasts', and the tip of the Siegessäule rising majestically from its centre. It was a panorama of German power and might capable of striking awe into anyone, let alone a schoolboy.

The rest of the first day was a free one for the touring party, a chance to acclimatize before a scheduled practice the next day and the first match on Friday the 6th. Their only appointment was lunch with the Berlin players at the Adlon, hosted and paid for by the Gents. They were all curious to meet the men who played a game that was ignored by the vast majority of their fellow countrymen. How had they become involved with the sport and why did they play it? they wondered. And just how good were they? Whatever they imagined, it's doubtful they could have guessed what a remarkable group of men the cricketers of Berlin were.

Lunch at the Adlon was a real treat for the Berlin players. It was also the first meeting between the Major and Felix Menzel. Despite their difference in nationality and class, did the two men recognize a common bond beyond a shared love of cricket? Both had worked tirelessly and selflessly to ensure the clubs they loved survived hardship – Worcestershire

CC in the impecunious post-war period in the Major's case, Preussen and the whole edifice of Berlin cricket under Nazi rule in Felix's.

Felix must have felt great pride as he sat and talked about the game with men of such cricketing pedigree. Three years earlier it had appeared the cricket oasis in Berlin might vanish. Yet here he was, in conversation with an English county cricketer, eating with one of the country's most celebrated amateur teams, ahead of a three-match series which he hoped would be the catalyst for a surge in interest in cricket among his compatriots. The dream which had its genesis at The Oval in the presence of Jack Hobbs had now grown into a vision. Felix imagined cricket spreading across Germany and the continent, reaching such a level of popularity that the MCC would send its finest players to take them on.

After lunch the English tourists visited the Neue Wache, the site of the 'Memorial for the Fallen of the War': a simple marble plinth backed by a cross bathed in a circle of light from a skylight above. It must have been a poignant time for those who had fought in that terrible conflict. The war still cast a long shadow – its consequences had created a void which Hitler had been only too willing to fill – but for the veterans on both sides these matches offered a chance to put the memories of those four years to rest.

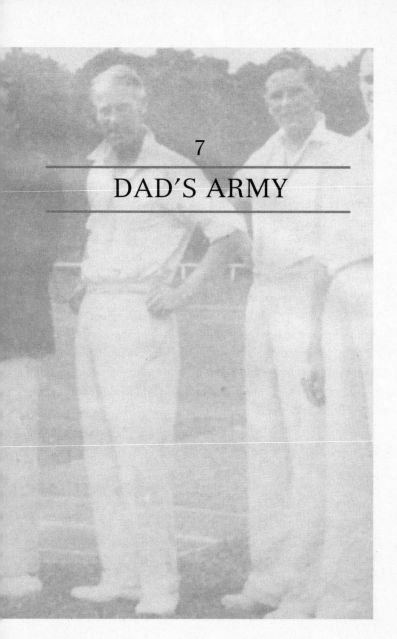

7

DAD'S ARMY

THE GENTS were not the sort to practise. Limbering up, nets, fielding practice – that sort of thing was best left to the professionals. Especially if the night before you'd been sampling the varied delights on offer at the Adlon's cocktail bar. But whether it was the cautionary words of Plum Warner or personal pride, the Gents rose from their beds earlier the next morning than some might have planned and rode a small fleet of taxis to the Berliner Sportvereins 92 club in Wilmersdorf to prepare for the first match.

BSV 92's ground was a football pitch. Even though it was surrounded by grassy slopes, which gave it the feel of a natural amphitheatre, the bumpy ground, patches of bare soil and long grass betrayed its main purpose. Worst of all was the thin matting pitch which the hosts had laid for their benefit. Some members of the team had had experience of artificial pitches in Denmark and the Netherlands so it was not entirely alien, but they were of a better quality than this. They had also been laid on grounds designated for cricket, or polo at the very least, not in the centre circle of a well-used football ground. But the Gents were not ones to complain. A smattering of press were at the ground to watch them practise and it would be discourteous to cause a fuss. The team changed into their whites and posed for a photograph before trekking out to the middle to test the conditions.

Not all of the squad were present. Robert Berkeley was missing, though the reason is a matter of conjecture.

According to his son the Captain was not the practising sort. 'He was probably off admiring the botanical gardens,' he wrote in an email when asked about his father's absence. Meanwhile Major Jewell's grandson said that his grandfather always reminded him of Captain Mainwaring in *Dad's Army*: the air of pomposity, the inability to suffer fools gladly or sadly while also fighting the sneaking suspicion that you were the fool, and the frustration that the world around you had gone to the dogs.

The Major had come into wealth via marriage rather than birth and, like Mainwaring, perhaps he envied those who moved with more ease in rarefied circles – men who were 'to the manner born' like Berkeley, who had inherited their own furniture (his family had slept in the same bed for four centuries after all). It's difficult not to cast Berkeley as Sergeant Wilson to the Major's Mainwaring: diffident, somewhat louche, more likely to inspect a garden the day before an important game than practise, while the Major eschewed such frivolity and put on his blazer and whites to prepare his boys, four eager Private Pikes among them, for a crucial match against the Jerries. After all, Britain didn't become Great by admiring flowers.

The other absent player was Robin Evelyn Whetherly. According to one German newspaper report, he joined them later that day after arriving by aeroplane. This would have involved boarding an Imperial Airways flight from Croydon Airport to Tempelhof, Berlin, via a stop at Amsterdam Schiphol, on a Handley Page 42, a four-engine biplane. While the Handley Page 42 was never involved in an accident in the whole time it was used by Imperial, it was a slow aircraft – the flight to Amsterdam took two hours, and it was a further three hours' flying from there to Berlin – and prone to turbulence (air travel would experience a surge in popularity after the war when comfort improved and air-sickness became less common). It was also the preserve of the wealthy: a return trip to Berlin in 1937 cost £18 and eight shillings, the equivalent of approximately £680 today.

Despite being a student at Oxford University, Whetherly was able to afford such an extravagance. A tall, dashing man with angular features, he came from a wealthy family. His father Lt Col William Stobart Whetherly was a decorated veteran of both the Boer War and the First World War as a member of the 7th Dragoon Guards and 19th Hussars respectively. Robin had been schooled at Harrow, where he proved to be a talented all-round sportsman. He represented the school at rugby and football but it was as wicketkeeper in the cricket eleven that he excelled. He played in two Eton v. Harrow games before moving up to Oxford, where he made the first XI in his second and third years. His glovework was excellent but he struggled with the bat. In the summer of 1937 he was coming to the end of his second year at Oxford and had played at The Parks against a touring New Zealand Test side. According to reports he was 'big, strong, brimming with confidence . . . a born leader'. He was also unafraid of a drunken jape or two. At one rugby club dinner Whetherly, 'feeling peckish towards midnight, led a charge with the roller from Cloisters, gathering speed to smash down the door into the kitchen in search of food . . . I dare say there were reprimands, and bills to pay.'

His skill with the gloves represented a coup for the Gents. In modern terms, he was a 'ringer'. The Gents often played one of their regulars in a makeshift role behind the stumps; Geoffrey Tomkinson occasionally did duty there, for instance. But Whetherly had never played for the Gents before and had no geographical connection with Worcestershire whatsoever. Before boarding at Harrow he had been born and raised in Kensington and Chelsea. Some of the players seem to have been equally mystified about who he was and where he came from. Peter Robinson said he was from 'Gloucestershire somewhere', though there is no link between the Whetherly clan and Gloucestershire either.

Whetherly attended Magdalen, the same Oxford college as Captain Berkeley. But as Berkeley graduated more than a decade before Whetherly arrived that seems an unlikely connection. Could there be another explanation for Whetherly's presence? He spoke German, presumably learned at Harrow because his degree was in history. And where did the funds come from to pay for his expensive flight to Berlin? Presumably his own pocket because it's unlikely that Major Jewell's largesse, already stretched by the presence of his son and three of his friends whose bills he was almost certainly covering, would go that far no matter how tidy Whetherly's keeping was. It's doubtful the Major would have flown even Les Ames out for that money. But it begs the question why he didn't choose to travel with the other members of the team.

Hunting, business and sporting trips were classic covers for minor espionage, mainly industrial espionage. Especially since Hitler had instructed his Abwehr not to spy on Britain in the period between 1935 and 1937, when tensions between the two nations were less pronounced. Therefore scrutiny of trips like the Gents tour was not as strict as one might imagine. The tourists were given freedom of passage into

Germany, though it's not certain if the same courtesy was extended to Whetherly when he flew in. It's possible, even likely, that one member of the team had been approached before the tour and asked to take note of what they saw and heard, and then, on his return, invited down to London 'for a chat, dear boy'. If so, given his fluency in German (and his later military career) there is a good chance that Whetherly was that man.

Ad hoc spy or not, his arrival that day completed the squad. He was too late to make the short practice session, which the matting wicket made 'jolly hard' according to Peter Robinson. There was genuine consternation that playing on a football field on an uneven rug might act as a leveller and offer the Berliners a glimmer of a chance. The Gents played their matches at Edgbaston and New Road, on public school pitches like Malvern College or Bromsgrove school, or on private grounds that all shared the same qualities: they were immaculately kept and flatter than a factory floor. Looking around at the rough outfield and long grass of the BSV 92 ground more suited to rugby than cricket, the Gents could be forgiven for thinking they were slumming it.

But if they were perturbed by the prospect, it didn't show. The first match of the tour beckoned but a cricket tour is a cricket tour, and there was no chance the Gents were going to be tucked up in bed by ten with a cup of cocoa. On one tour, in Guernsey, the Major had got so drunk that he'd tried to start a fight with his own reflection as he staggered past a hallway mirror on his way to bed. He had been much younger in those days, but while their best hell-raising days were behind them, some still enjoyed the odd glass or several.

The entire team booked a fleet of taxis and headed to Potsdamer Platz, less than a mile south of their hotel. The quickest route was via Hermann Göring Strasse,* which ran south from the Brandenburg Gate to Potsdamer Platz, but the road, named after the preening, strutting Nazi Reichsmarschall whose residence was nearby, had been closed after a series of accidents. The street had been dug up before the 1936 Olympics to build a link for the S-Bahn between the Unter den Linden and Yorkstrasse. In their eagerness to have the tunnel ready in time for the Games safety measures were ignored and in 1935 part of it collapsed, burying twenty-three workmen in the rubble. Only four were found alive. Then in 1936 a fire near Potsdamer Platz destroyed much of the construction equipment on site. So their taxis took them down Wilhelmstrasse, the broad avenue which represented the centre of Nazi power in Berlin, past the Chancellery and the balcony where Hitler stood to wave at adoring crowds, and the headquarters of Rudolf Hess, Hitler's deputy, before turning right along Potsdamer Strasse just before the Reich Air Ministry, where Göring was overseeing the rapid expansion of the Luftwaffe in preparation for war.

If Wilhelmstrasse was the dark core of Nazi power, then Potsdamer Platz was the metropolis's neon heart. The lights from its hotels, bars, restaurants, department stores

---

* The road is known now as Eberstrasse and is the site of the vast memorial to those killed in the Holocaust. Between 1961 and 1989 the Berlin Wall ran along its entire length.

and streetlamps blazed brighter than Piccadilly Circus. Five different streets met to form a star-shaped intersection which was the hub of the city. Traffic roared through day and night and people flocked to be there, to feel at the heart of it, even if its pleasures were often beyond their means.

That was not a problem for the Gents. Their destination that evening wasn't just a restaurant. Haus Vaterland was a pleasure palace the size of a department store: for an entrance fee of one Deutschmark, people had access to a vast complex spread across six floors containing a range of restaurants, a café, cabaret, amusement arcades, a concert hall and a cinema. It was 'a perfectly planned city of entertainment' according to German writer Franz Hessel. 'Die Welt in einem Haus' ('the world in one place') promised its promotional literature, and it came heartily recommended by most contemporary tourist guides. 'I can think of no better way to top off a Berlin night . . . than an hour or two or three in Haus Vaterland. The place is . . . the very essence of Berlin,' enthused Sydney Clark in *Germany on £10* in 1934.

A sort of proto-Disneyland for adults, its twelve themed restaurants were inspired by different parts of the world. There was a Wild West Bar, which re-created a saloon complete with swinging doors and waiters in ten-gallon hats. In a flyer written at the time and translated for English-speaking guests (and salvaged as a souvenir by Peter Robinson) the bar is described thus: 'This odd room in the style of a blockhouse makes you feel like being way-out in the real prairie. You will find whisky bottles standing on the tables and of course there is music, and the American songs and melodies sung just like across the big pond.' Apparently the owners allowed an American room but forbade a French or British one because they couldn't forgive either country for the stringent terms of the Treaty of Versailles.

Other rooms included the Grinzing in an Austrian theme, complete with a model railway that threaded its way around the room, travelling on bridges over a re-creation of the Danube. The Löwenbräu was a facsimile of a giant Bavarian beer garden where buxom waitresses served a thousand people while bands and musicians serenaded the guests. Those seeking more exotic or less bawdy treats could eat and drink in a Spanish Bodega, a Turkish Café, a Hungarian Csarda or the Japanese Tea-room. The crowning glory was the Rheinterrasse, a cavernous hall decorated with a seventy-foot-wide panorama of the Rhine countryside and surrounded by a miniature river which flowed around the edges of the room. On every hour the lights would dim to denote a darkening sky, a fake roar of thunder would echo around the room, hidden fans would blow a stiff breeze and 'rain' would sprinkle on the diners below, before a battery of lights were switched on to re-create a sunburst after the storm. During this display a group of scantily clad 'Rhine maidens' danced seductively between the tables. Then there was the ballroom, based on the Garden of Eden and decorated with palm fronds and silver sculptures, where the 'Vaterland Girls' performed regular shows.

It really did put the kitsch in kitchen . . . and Haus Vaterland's kitchen was the biggest in the world, capable of catering for a staggering eight thousand people. It had opened in the last days of Weimar Germany and quickly become a place to see and be seen. One million paying customers passed through its front door in the first year it was open. Unsurprisingly given its cosmopolitan clientele and decadent image the Nazis were not fans, but they also knew on which side their pumpernickel was buttered. The Vaterland was a Berlin institution for residents and visitors with money to spend, so it was tolerated – though its Jewish owners, the Kempinski family, were forced to sell the place to 'Aryan' owners for a pittance and fled the country.

The original owners may have been forced into exile but the fun continued. The Vaterland acted as a metaphor for much of Nazi Berlin. On the surface day-to-day life carried on as it had always done, albeit draped with Nazi flags and symbols and periodic displays and parades of power. But behind the veil daily life was punctuated by brutality and humiliation. Those Jews who had not fled Berlin had been stripped of their businesses and their pride, condemned to live as third-class citizens, while thousands of enemies of the state had been thrown into concentration camps and thousands more lived in fear of the same fate.

Across Potsdamer Platz from the Haus Vaterland stood the gleaming Columbushaus, a nine-storey modernist shopping and office block. Built in 1932, it became a symbol of German modernism and prosperity and the giant neon sign on its roof advertising the *Braune Post*, a Nazi newspaper, had become one of the city's most famous landmarks. But it held a dark secret behind its gleaming exterior. The Gestapo had taken over the top floors and turned them into a prison where the SS interrogated and tortured those deemed to be a threat to internal security. Men were stripped and beaten senseless or whipped. The journalist Kurt Hiller was taken there and had his nose and teeth broken. Then he was laid on a wooden table and given fifty lashes until his back and buttocks were a bloody mess. Then he was forced to stand in a prison cell, and if he flagged he was dragged outside and asked to do a humiliating dance while singing children's songs as the guards looked on and laughed. His kidneys were damaged, his legs started to swell, and despite advice from a doctor to allow him to rest on a bed he was forced to carry out this gruesome dance regularly until finally he collapsed in excruciating pain. His crime had been to write for a leftist magazine that had a circulation of just fifteen thousand. He would survive, but millions of others didn't.*

The Gents were oblivious to this. Inside the Vaterland they drank, they danced and they played. Peter Robinson, thrilled to be let loose in such a place at such a tender age, was mesmerized. 'I just had the best steak and onions I have had a la carte,' he gushed to his parents in a postcard. Heaven knows what they would have made of it had they known he was writing about one of the most notorious nightclubs in Berlin. 'Then there were various rooms with music and dancing and setting representing certain countries. Terry and I thought the "Wild West Bar" was the best! We spent a lot on amusements, such as shooting and handle-football. Terry and I had at least 12 matches of the last (Leeds Utd v Derby).'

While two of the youngest team members played table football, the rest of the squad enjoyed more grown-up pleasures before heading home to sleep.

---

* At some stage in the 1930s – the exact date is unknown – the Gestapo moved their operation out of Columbushaus. But the building's link with evil was not severed. In 1939 the Nazis rented office space where they planned the execution of the physically and mentally handicapped.

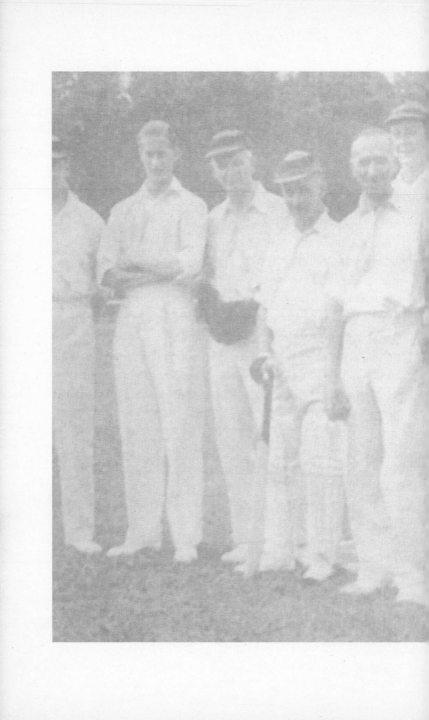

8

PROPAGANDA FÜR KRICKET

On Friday, 6 August 1937, the sun shone over Berlin. Back in Britain the fascist newspaper *Blackshirt* fulminated about Jewish refugees from Germany taking teaching positions while 'British teachers walked the streets looking for jobs'; the *Times* correspondent in the German capital noted without alarm that Göring was calling for small craftsmen and shopkeepers to join the programme of 'rearmament and industrial development'; Cowes Regatta came to a close; and in the absence of their Master, the Berkeley Foxhounds appeared in the ring at Tring Show. In Wilmersdorf, the Gentlemen of Worcestershire played the first match of their tour.

The squad arrived at the ground in taxis for an 11.30 start one player short. Not the mysterious Robin Whetherly again but Cyril Smith, who had to stay behind in bed at the Adlon. This wasn't the consequence of over-indulgence at Haus Vaterland the night before but the result of a fever caused, he believed, by leaving that cabin window open all night on the Nord-Express to Berlin. His absence meant that Peter Robinson, brought along as twelfth man and general dogsbody, would get a game. Smith's pugnacious batting in the middle order would be missed but as their opposition for this game was a Berlin 2nd XI they were not too worried. The side was led by Gerhard Thamer, who had been on the 1930 tour of England and whose father was part of the first German side to play England at football, in 1901. The intention was to give the lesser lights of Berlin cricket a chance to compete against a crack English team while allowing the visitors to accustom themselves to the conditions ahead of sterner tests.

By eleven o'clock a healthy if unspectacular crowd had trickled through the turnstiles. Many were Berlin cricketers, past and present, including the Menzel brothers and other players who would be turning out in the two-day game starting the next day. Those not involved with Berlin's cricket scene had been lured in by a combination of the previews printed in the local press and the promise of free entry. *Das Fußball-Megaphon* led its latest edition, published on the morning of the first match, with an idiot's guide to the game complete with a rather laborious description of its rules, which was surely enough to smother the curiosity of even the most ardent Berlin sport lover. Things picked up a bit in a short article praising English sporting teams and their 'gallant fighting spirit, their camaraderie and their discipline'. 'The English Cricket players are in Berlin! They want to help promote the sport, to make it attractive for our youth,' they added.

Die Fußball-Woche displayed a unique grasp of English geography by billing the fixture as 'Berlin v London'. The hyperbole did not end there. 'There are 5 county players; they are more or less all-star players,' it gushed about the Gents team. 'If you could compare this sport to football, they would have been considered for the national team – and played for the national team – multiple times!' The magazine exhorted its readers to watch the matches. 'Those who make the trip to Schmargendorf, the Tib-field and the Maifeld will not be disappointed, as the German–English matches will showcase the most formidable art of Cricket. We cannot predict how well the team from Berlin will play. The English are clearly the favourites to win, even though in these venues the game is played on matting which the English team is not used to playing on.' *FuWo* had also learned that in the previous week's round of county championship matches Dick Moore of Hampshire and Lancashire's Eddie Paynter had scored triple centuries on the same day. 'Here we are happy when one player scores 80 runs,' it noted, rather forlornly.

The daily newspapers also ran previews. Under the headline 'Propaganda Für Kricket', the *Berlin Tageblatt** tried to decode the popular appeal of cricket in England for its readers. 'For the Englishman who does not play tennis, row or go to the races, this is the only summer sport that makes him happy,' their correspondent wrote. He was also pessimistic about the chances of the Berlin side. 'The skill of the English players exceeds the skill of the Germans by far,' he continued, before adding, 'Even without the big stars, who stayed at home to continue playing their main season, the team will be good enough to support the representatives from Berlin in promoting this beautiful game.'

Predictably the NSDAP's official newspaper, *Volkische Beobachter*, was more bullish about the home team's prospects, even if they recognized the superior pedigree of the tourists. 'The English have cancelled two other guest matches to be able to play in Berlin. The fact that they are playing for free and are financing their own stay is a very

---

* The *Tageblatt* had been an extremely influential liberal newspaper. Even when the Nazis seized control of all press in 1933 in order to give the impression they ran a free press, they allowed the paper some independence rather than using it as a propaganda mouthpiece. The relationship was always an uneasy one, however, and it was eventually closed in early 1939.

friendly gesture towards the German sports world. Given the exceptional strength and expertise of the guests we can look forward to great performances and exciting matches. It will be difficult for the German teams, who have prepared themselves by playing training matches, to hold the experienced opponents at bay or to win against them. We can, however, expect the Berlin teams to fight courageously and achieve a good result.'

The Gents changed into their whites. Despite the previous day's practice they were not the sort to undergo pre-match warm-ups. Four of the team were over forty and two of them had reached their half centuries; their idea of preparation was to smear some Elliman's Athletic Rub on their war wounds (literally, in some cases) and smoke a cigarette or two. But the lads were keen to practise so the venerable Geoffrey Tomkinson, then in his fifty-sixth year, agreed to hit them some catches on the outfield. He did this in the time-honoured way, by lobbing a cricket ball in the air with one hand then smacking it with a bat held in the other while the young bucks took it in turn to try and catch the skyers.

The Berlin team stopped their preparations to watch. They were amazed, not by the catching of the young Englishmen but by Tomkinson's one-handed hitting. To their eyes he seemed able to hit the ball high and far without any effort. Just a flick of the wrist and a crack of the bat and the ball soared into the azure sky before completing a slow descent. A few of them even felt moved to applaud each hit.

Tomkinson was a big hitter, in every sense. Off the field

he was chairman of Tomkinsons Ltd of Kidderminster, one of the most famous carpet firms in the country. He was awarded an OBE for his services to British industry and later knighted. During the First World War he had served with the Worcestershire Regiment and reached the rank of Lieutenant Colonel, was twice wounded, Mentioned in Dispatches and earned the Military Cross. He'd served on Kidderminster Town Council for fifteen years and was made Mayor in 1929.

On the field he had enjoyed a singular first-class cricket career. After impressing at Winchester College and Cambridge he was selected to play for Worcestershire against his own university in 1903. He scored 1 in his only innings. Once he graduated he moved to Brazil where he worked as an engineer on the Great Western Railway until the outbreak of war. When he left the Army in 1919 he joined the family firm and started to play cricket for Kidderminster in the Birmingham League. He had lost none of his talents and at the age of forty-five was recalled to the county side for a match against Derbyshire, more than twenty-three years after his debut. He scored 10 and 1, and there his first-class career ended.

But he continued to write his name into Midlands cricket legend as the most feared free-scoring batsman in the Birmingham League. His achievements reflect his aggressive batting style: in separate innings he scored a double century in two hours, a century in twenty-five minutes, and once struck fifty-two runs off two (six-ball) overs. Together with one of the most curious first-class careers in cricket history he could also lay claim to the biggest six ever hit. A railway track runs parallel to the Kidderminster ground and one six

Fisher, zeigte mir persönlich sein New College und führte
mich auch auf die umfangreichen sportlichen Anlagen, die
für das College zur Verfügung stehen. Bei dieser Gelegenheit konnte ich mich davon überzeugen, in welch großem Maße
hier sportliche Übungsstätten sowohl für die Studierenden
der einzelnen Colleges als auch für die gesamte Studenten-
schaft geschaffen sind und in welch hervorragender Verfassung
sie sich befinden.

Des weiteren hatte ich Gelegenheit, ein bedeutendes Polo-
Spiel in Hurlingham, in dem für die Entwicklung des Polo-
sports maßgebenden Klub, sowie Cricket Spiele auf den
historischen Lord's Cricket Grounds, die man als "Mekka"
des englischen Cricket Sports bezeichnen kann, zu sehen.

Die Boys'Clubs, die ich besuchte, sind eine vor mehreren
Jahren geschaffene Einrichtung für die körperliche Betäti-
gung der Jugend der ärmeren Stadtteile. Die Einrichtung
dieser Boys'Clubs zeichnet sich durch den Willen einzelner,
für dies soziale Problem interessierter Kreise aus, läßt
sich aber in keiner Weise vergleichen mit der umfassenden
Fürsorge und Gesamterziehung, die durch die HJ bei uns
jeden Jungen und jedes Mädchen erfaßt.

Ich hatte insbesondere Gelegenheit, mich mit de...
der Studienkommission englischer Er...
ihre Erfahrungen in Deu...
der Studienk...
der kö...
allen ...
auch in...
ständnis...

Ostende La Malle « Prince Baudouin ».
Oostende De Maiboot

Top Lord's was the 'Mekka' of English cricket, according to Tschammer und Osten's report for Hitler.

Right The *Prince Baudouin*, which ferried the Worcestershire Gents to and from Ostend.

Above The sumptuous Adlon, one of Europe's finest hotels, and the Gents' home for their eight days in Berlin.

Below The local weekly *Das Fußball-Megaphon* welcomes the Gents.

Das Fußball-Megaphon

Fußball-Vorschau für alle Berliner Gauliga- und Bezirksklassenspiele

Nachdruck nur mit Quellenangabe gestattet. Erfüllungsort und Gerichtsstand: In jedem Falle Berlin-Mitte. Zuschriften, welche die Redaktion betreffen, sind nur an den Verlag Emil Wernitz & Co., Berlin N 65, Müllerstr. 10, zu richten. Fernsprecher: 46 67 47/49. Postscheckkonto: Berlin 654 97. Erscheint zu jedem Gauliga- und Bezirksklassenspiel. Preis: 0,10 RM.

10. Jahrgang	Berlin, 6.—12. August 1937	Nummer 25

Willkommen, Worcestershire!

Englische Sportleute sind wieder in Deutschland. Immer, wenn die „old boys" deutschen Boden betraten, haben sie durch ihr faires, vorbildliches Verhalten, durch ihre ritterliche Kampfesweise, durch ihre Kameradschaft und Selbstdisziplin die Herzen der deutschen Zuschauer erobert. Wir haben es erlebt, als englische Vereinsmannschaften unseren Fußballvertretungen harte und erbitterte Kämpfe lieferten, die halbe Welt war Zeuge, als die englische Fußball-Nationalelf damals im alten Grunewaldstadion jenes unvergeßliche 3:3-Spiel gegen die deutsche Amateurklasse bestritt. Aber laßt uns nicht nur vom Fußball reden. Auch in den anderen Sportarten, in der Leicht-

voreiligen Meinung und auch ungerechtfertigten Voreingenommenheit hat es der Cricketsport zu verdanken, daß trotz 40jähriger Tätigkeit deutscher Cricketvereine das Spiel die Formen und Ausmaße wie beispielsweise beim Fußball nicht annehmen konnte. Aber im gleichen Atemzuge muß den Männern ein hohes Lob gesungen werden, die immer und immer wieder trotz mannigfacher Schwierigkeiten für Cricket warben und Cricket spielten. Nur ihrer Beständigkeit, ihrer zähen Beharrlichkeit ist es zuzuschreiben, daß das deutsche Cricket auch im Auslande immer noch Geltung hat.

Englands Cricketer weilen in Berlin! Sie wollen

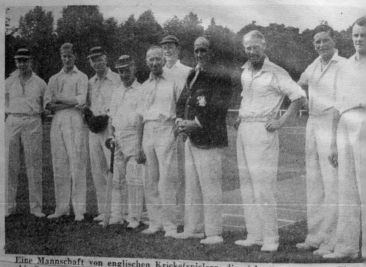

chaft- und Forschungs... der II spielte mit gutem Verständnis für den BSV.

Eine Mannschaft von englischen Kricketspielern, die sich „Gentlemen von Worce... shire" nennen, weilen zurzeit in Berlin. Sie gewannen ihre ersten beiden Spiel... der Reichshauptstadt in großem Stil. Unser Bild zeigt die sympathischen Gäste... alle jeder Zoll ein gentleman

Bild von Schirner, Ber...

...enn man den Engländer fragt, was das typischste ...le Spiel sei, so wird er nicht sagen: Fußball, ... Kricket." ...England besitzt das Spiel ...

Above The Gents before their first practice: (*from left to right*) Smith, Terry, Tomkinson, Williams, Anton, Huntington-Whiteley, Major Jewell, Deeley, Maurice Jewell, Robinson.

Right Dickie Williams practises on the bumpy matting pitch. Geoffrey Tomkinson stands in as keeper in Robin Whetherly's absence.

6. August 1937 ∗ Nr. 218 ∗ Seite 11

Englands Kricketer beim Abschlußtraining für den heute gegen Brandenburgs Gaumannschaft stattfindenden Kampf auf dem BSV-Platz (Beginn 10.30 Uhr)

Aufn.: Schirner

Ullmann schoß Weltrekord
Deutsche Schützen schlecht „in Schuß"

Above The Major strikes the ball at the intrepid photographer at short mid-off.

Below But the snapper gets the last laugh as the Major is bowled by Thamer.

Left The photographer appears to have got even closer to take this photo of Peter Terry at the crease.

Below Wetherly behind the stumps as an unnamed Berlin batsman attempts a rather curious late cut.

511:198 für die En

Der meisterhafte Wicketkeeper der Engländer, Wetherly, bei der „Arbeit". Seinen riesigen Händen entglitt kaum ein Ball.
Bild: Hohmann, Berlin

Left This photo, taken in 1931, shows 'Mauschel' Schmidt in mid-delivery. Felix Menzel looks on from the non-striker's end.

Left Peter Robinson's official invitation from the Nazi Sports Ministry to the end-of-tour dinner.

Below An aerial view of the Olympiastadion complex where the last match was played, though Schenkendorf-platz is not shown.

Below The signatures of Young Maurice, Peter Huntington-Whiteley, Dickie Williams, William Deeley, Peter Terry and the Major, collected by Peter Robinson.

Above and below Robinson's collection
of signatures of the German players and officials,
gathered at the dinner marking the end of the tour.

MY SCORES:-
2, 2, 0, 2 not out, 2.
Average 2.
Caught 4 Catches.
Missed, 4 Catches.

Left Robinson's rather damning statistical summary of his tour.

Below The Gents toured so regularly they even had their own baggage labels.

WORCESTERSHIRE GENTLEMEN'S
P. E. B. ROBINSON,
HIGHLEY,
UPTON-ON-SE
WORCS.
VIA OSTEND, DOVER & PADDINGTON.
ENGLAND.

Below Captain Berkeley's account of the tour for the *Cricketer Annual* of 1937, including scorecards of all three matches.

The Gentlemen of Worcestershire in Berlin

THE Gentlemen of Worcestershire went to Berlin during August for their annual foreign tour. Although the standard of cricket, as played by the Germans, is not quite on a par with the Dutch or the Danes, their hospitality was unbounded, and the tour will remain one of most pleasant memories.

From the time that the side left Victoria Station until the return, everything possible was done, beginning with a " Laissez Passee " from the German Embassy which spared us many inconveniences, such as being woken up at the frontier, in the middle of the night, for the always tedious Customs examination. At the early hour of 8 a.m. the XI. arrived in Berlin to find on the station a large gathering of German sportsmen. Numerous cinema and Press cameras were also in evidence.

This tour was all the more interesting because it was only the second occasion that an English cricket team had visited Germany. Three two-day matches were played, one of which was at the magnificent Olympic arena, where Signor Mussolini recently addressed three million people.

Cricket in Germany is played on matting wickets, and all the grounds we played on were either State or Municipal Sports Grounds. The batting of the Germans was decidedly weak, owing to a lack of coaching, but it is hoped that the Reichsport Führer will give permission for an English professional to go to Berlin next year. This will make a vast difference to the standard of cricket. Cricket cannot be learnt from a book; tuition and practice are essential. The bowling of Herr Felix Menzel and Herr G. Menzel is almost Veritian in steadiness; and it is

remarkable how these two cricketers can bowl for three or four hours on end without losing their length. They both bowl medium-pace right-hand almost entirely on the leg-stump, just short of a length. The field is placed as follows—no slips, no cover, no extra cover, and a vast concourse of fieldsmen on the leg-side. The fielding is decidedly good, and in this respect special mention should be made of Herr Lehmann, who is particularly brilliant in any position.

The young German players in Germany require coaching and encouragement, and some of the rather drastic punishment that is on occasions meted out to them when catches are missed could, with advantage to the game, be discontinued. A dropped catch, after all, is a mistake which anyone would avoid if possible, and is never done on purpose!!

Mention must be made of R. H. Williams' century, which was the first ever made in German cricket, and cf Major Jewell's 140, which was the highest ever made against the Germans.

The Reichsports Führer honoured the Gentlemen of Worcestershire by his presence at two of the matches, entertaining us to tea and attending the final banquet.

On several occasions official Government cars were placed at the disposal of the side and we were taken to many functions and sight-seeing expeditions on "off" days.

Altogether it was a most enjoyable and memorable tour, and it is greatly to be hoped that other English sides will visit Berlin. Should the Germans ever send a side to England they can be quite certain that they will be most welcome guests, especially to the Gentlemen of Worcestershire.   R. B.

GENTLEMEN OF WORCESTERSHIRE v. A BERLIN XI.
Played at B.S.V. Ground, Berlin, August 6, 1937. Gentlemen of Worcestershire won by 101 runs.

GENTLEMEN OF WORCESTERSHIRE

M. F. S. Jewell, c Pfitzner, b Thamer	14	
R. H. Williams, b Thamer	1	c Madder, b Thamer ... 9
P. N. L. Terry, lbw, b Menzke	5	c Behnke, b Thamer ... 7
R. G. Berkeley, b Thamer	3	b Dartsch ... 17
R. E. Whetherly, lbw, b Thamer	1	not out ... 57
M. Jewell, c Dartsch, b Menzke	52	not out ... 4
W. Deeley, st Behnke, b Menzke	11	
G. S. Tomkinson, c Menzke, b Thamer	16	
C. S. Anton, not out	11	
P. F. B. Robinson, b Menzke	2	
H. O. Huntington-Whiteley, b Menzke	26	lbw, b Thamer ... 2
Extras	1	Extras ... 6
Total	**117**	**Total (4 wkts.) ... 118**

A BERLIN XI

Behnke, b H.-Whiteley	4	c Jewell, b H.-Whiteley ... 1
Dartsch, b H.-Whiteley	4	b Jewell ... 8
Mader, b Deeley	1	c Robinson, b Anton ... 9
Dartsch, b Deeley	3	b Anton ... 2
Thamer, c Robinson, b H.-Whiteley	0	c Terry, b Jewell ... 6
Lehmann, c Williams, b Jewell	8	b Anton ... 3
Menzke, c Whetherly, b Jewell	0	not out ... 10
Gruhn, b Jewell	7	c Deeley, b Williams ... 20
Dietz, b Anton	10	b Williams ... 5
Zickert, b Jewell	2	c Whetherly, b Williams ... 13
Pfitzner, not out	1	c Whetherly, b Jewell ... 4
Extras	14	Extras ... 4
Total	**62**	**Total ... 72**

GENTLEMEN OF WORCESTERSHIRE v. BERLIN.
Played at Tilt-Platz. Gentlemen of Worcestershire won by 113 runs.

GENTLEMEN OF WORCESTERSHIRE

M. F. S. Jewell, c Maus, b F. Menzel	1	not out ... 10
R. H. Williams, lbw, b G. Menzel	40	b G. Menzel ... 104
P. N. L. Terry, b F. Menzel	22	c F. Menzel, b G. Menzel ... 6
R. G. Berkeley, c Mader, b F. Menzel	15	b Thamer ... 28
R. E. Whetherly, lbw, b F. Menzel	6	lbw, b Thamer ... 29
M. Jewell, c Lehmann, b F. Menzel	12	c Zehmke, b F. Menzel ... 2
W. Deeley, c Lehmann, b F. Menzel	64	c Parnemann, b Thamer ... 29
G. S. Tomkinson, b Anton	54	c sub., b Thamer ... 6
C. S. Anton, lbw, b F. Menzel	4	b Reiss ... 19
H. O. Huntington-Whiteley, not out	16	b G. Menzel ... 2
P. E. B. Robinson, run out	4	lbw, b Thamer ... 8
Extras	13	Extras ... 8
Total	**271**	**Total ... 240**

BERLIN

Maus	b Ancon ... 35
Parnemann	b Anton ... 45
Mader	c Williams, b Deeley ... 9
F. Dartsch	b Anton ... 2
Reiss	b Jewell ... 2
Zehmke	b Anton ... 6
G. Menzel	b Anton ... 3
Anton	c Jewell, b Deeley ... 5
Thamer	c M. Jewell, b M. F. S. Jewell ... 28
F. Menzel	not out ... 17
Ludwig	b Williams ... 17
B. Dartsch	Extras ... 9
	Total ... 150

Details of first innings not available

GENTLEMEN OF WORCESTERSHIRE v. BERLIN.
Played at Olympic Stadium, August 10 and 11, 1937. Gentlemen of Worcestershire won by 249 runs.

GENTLEMEN OF WORCESTERSHIRE

R. H. Williams, b F. Menzel	41	not out ... 6
M. F. S. Jewell, c Dartsch, b G. Menzel	140	
P. N. L. Terry, c Parnemann, b F. Menzel	2	
R. E. Whetherly, c and b Thamer	17	not out ... 16
M. Jewell, c Maus, b Thamer	10	c Parnemann, b F. Menzel ... 13
W. Deeley, c Thamer, b Parnemann	5	c Mader, b G. Menzel ... 18
G. S. Tomkinson, c and b F. Menzel	15	b G. Menzel ... 18
C. S. Anton, c Dartsch, b F. Menzel	1	c Thamer, b F. Menzel ... 18
H. H.-Whiteley, b G. Menzel	5	b F. Menzel ... 0
Herr Lehmann, b F. Menzel	13	b G. Menzel ... 0
P. Robinson, not out	2	b F. Menzel ... 8
Extras	—	Extras ... 4
Total	**265**	**Total (8 wkts. decd.) ... 39**

BERLIN

Parnemann, run out	2	c M. Jewell, b H.-Whiteley ... 4
Maus, c Whetherly, b H.-Whiteley	4	b H.-Whiteley ... 6
Mader, b Deeley	2	c Terry, b Jewell ... 1
Riets, b H.-Whiteley	0	c Terry, b Jewell ... 4
G. Menzel, b Anton	21	c Terry, b Jewell ... 2
Thamer, b Deeley	2	b Tomkinson ... 2
Dartsch, not out	6	c Whetherly, b Jewell ... 5
Zehmke, c M. F. S. Jewell, b Anton	0	b Terry ... 4
F. Menzel, c M. Jewell, b Deeley	0	b H.-Whiteley, b Jewell ... 4
Gruhn, c Lehmann, b Anton	0	c Terry, b Jewell ... 0
Zickert, b Deeley	4	not out ... 0
Extras	—	Extras ... 4
Total	**56**	**Total ... 39**

of Tomkinson's landed in the carriage of a passing goods train on its way to Cardiff – a distance of 105 miles. On another occasion he hit a ball so far it cleared the railway line and plugged in an allotment. Three days later, when the allotment owner was turning over his topsoil, he found the lost ball, which he gifted to a neighbour's child. When word got back to the Kidderminster CC chairman the unfortunate gardener was charged with stealing a cricket ball, found guilty in a magistrates court and fined thirteen shillings.

Once the hands of the young Gents had been warmed, Tomkinson ended his hitting exhibition. The Gentlemen of Worcestershire's captain, Major Maurice Jewell, and his opposite number, Gerhard Thamer, went to toss. It is not known who won or lost but the Gents were given, or chose, the dubious honour of first use of the matting pitch. Before the match began, however, there was a local custom to attend to. Not wishing to upset their hosts, the Gents were keen to be courteous, even if the custom was a strange one.

Shortly before the scheduled start of 11.30 a.m. all twenty-two cricketers, dressed in their whites, stood in a line facing one another on the outfield. Once in place Thamer shouted, 'Worcestershire Gentlemen, Sieg . . .'

'Heil!' barked the rest of the Berlin team in perfect unison, their arm raised in salute to their Führer, Adolf Hitler.

Now it was the visitors' turn. The Major cleared his throat, and in rather less strident tones than his opposite number said, 'Berlin CC, Sieg . . .'

'Heil,' came the rather uncertain response from his men.

There was no fuss over this gesture – a world away from the football international between England and Germany at the Olympic Stadium the following year when the question

127

of whether or not the England players would offer the salute whipped up a diplomatic kerfuffle. Allegedly under orders from the British ambassador in Berlin, Neville Henderson, and the Football Association, the players, including Stanley Matthews, were told to give the salute as a mark of respect. The turmoil and handwringing that resulted turned out to be pointless because Hitler did not even show up to watch the game, which England won 6–3. But the image of the team, their right arms raised, still has resonance today because we know what was lurking around the corner. The match was also covered by radio and the world's press. Not so for the Gents. For them it was simply a question of good manners, though they must have felt some unease because they neglected to mention it after the war. The Gents would claim that whenever someone offered them the Nazi salute they responded by lifting their hats, which indicates a desire to rewrite history somewhat. Before condemning the Gents for their compliance, however, it's worth considering that they toured during a comparatively benign period of Nazi rule. By May 1938, when England's footballers played their match, German troops had marched into Austria and Hitler's aggressive expansionist plans had been exposed to the world.

Supplementing the pack of reporters and photographers who had arrived to cover the day's play were a film crew who were keen to follow every step of the Gents' preparation. The Gents were to bat first, and their batsmen retreated to the dressing rooms to pad up – followed by the film crew. It was only when one of the senior batsmen rolled down his trousers and removed his 'box' from his bag, the sort with 'straps galore' which tied around the waist, that someone decided it might be wise to call 'Cut!'

The Major and Dickie Williams were the openers. As they walked out to the middle they were joined by a photographer. This certainly never happened at country house matches back in Blighty! The two men smiled politely, bade each other good luck, and the Major prepared to take strike. His opposite number Thamer, a slight, humourless blond-haired man, was to open the bowling with his gentle seamers.

As he glanced around, the Major was surprised to see the field Thamer had set. A mid-off, no one in the covers, no slips, and the rest ranged in a vast semi-circle behind and in front of square on the leg side. For a brief second he must have thought he was facing his old teammate Fred Root. Perhaps Thamer was a skilled exponent of inswing? The closest man to him on the offside was the photographer, who had taken up a position at short extra cover. He stayed there, camera poised, as Thamer marked out his short run and turned to bowl the first ball of the match. There was a pause as the bewildered Major waited for the photographer to leave the field until it was explained to him that he would be staying to capture the start of play. The Major interpreted this to mean the first few balls would be for show: he would pat back a few deliveries, the photographer would take his pictures, then he would get off the pitch and the match would start in earnest. But the Germans insisted that any play was for real and the photographer would remain on the field until he was satisfied he had the shots he needed. The Major didn't know it was common practice in Berlin for photographers to be allowed on the field during play. (Indeed, on their trip to Berlin in 1930 the *FuWo* correspondent had commented with some surprise on the English propensity to treat cricket grounds as sacred places: 'How it must be cared for and guarded! Nobody except those in play is allowed to step on the field, not even photographers.') Ever the courteous guest, and unwilling to cause a scene, the Major relented. Thamer bowled the first ball and the tour was officially underway.

There's no doubt the presence of the photographer disturbed the Major's concentration. The photographs, printed in the state's official sport magazine *Reichssportblatt* no less, show his brow furrowed in anger. In one image the ball seems to have been struck towards the photographer, which would confirm a story told by Young Maurice that the photographer limped off after being hit on the leg by a fierce cover drive – which may or may not have been an accident. However, another photograph shows the Major being bowled while attempting an extravagant drive, and it's taken from the same position as the first, which suggests that anger got the better of the Major and his desire to teach the impudent photographer a lesson might have been his downfall.

The scorecard states that the Major was out caught, but the photo proves otherwise. In the absence of an independent scorer – one of Peter Robinson's tasks had Cyril Smith been well enough to play – the players were doing it themselves, and as any amateur cricketer will confirm, often those playing are the least likely to be paying close attention to play on the field.*

* A word here about the scorecards from this tour. Put simply, they don't add up. Several different versions seem to have survived, though not the scorebook itself. I have taken the scorecards published in the *Cricketer Annual 1937* as the definitive version because they were supplied by Captain Berkeley, who presumably had the scorebook. But many of the innings confound any efforts to make them tally mathematically, this first innings of the tour being a case in point.

The Major's dismissal for 14 left the Gents in trouble. Thamer had already removed Dickie Williams, Robert Berkeley and Robin Whetherly cheaply, while the bowler at the other end, Willi Mesecke, had trapped Peter Terry lbw for a duck on his Gents debut. Half the team were out with twenty runs on the board and embarrassment beckoned. Salvation came in the form of Young Maurice who came in at 6 and hit 57. He was given support by the experienced trio of William Deeley, Geoffrey Tomkinson and Charles 'C. S.' Anton, a Scots-born (Private Frazer perhaps?) all-rounder who owned Victoria Carpets, competitors of Tomkinsons. Despite their business rivalry, Anton and Tomkinson were good friends and played together for Kidderminster as well as the Gents.

Maurice was eventually caught off Mesecke's bowling by Bruno Dartsch, an Army sergeant who had been granted leave to play. Mesecke and Thamer bowled uninterrupted throughout the whole Gents innings, taking five wickets apiece, though a useful last-wicket stand between Peters Two and Three, Huntington-Whiteley and Robinson, held the Berliners up before the Gents were dismissed for 147 – according to Robinson's letter at least (the scorecard claims they scored 117, but that cannot be the case). Given their shaky start, this represented a good recovery and showed the Gents' batting depth. Robinson aside, the batting order could be pulled from a hat without weakening it.

The presence of a photographer in the infield was not the Gents' only culture shock. Just as disconcerting was the habitual cry of 'Aus!' from the whole fielding side, including the man at long leg, whenever the ball struck a batsman on the pad and was in the same postcode as the stumps. The

Gents were of a generation and culture that appealed only for certainties, and even then it was only the job of the bowler and the wicketkeeper – perhaps first slip too if he was feeling bold – to make the enquiry. So to encounter a team that went up in unison at every opportunity came as a surprise to say the least. The Gents came to the conclusion it was all part of a plan to unsettle them at the crease – another tactic they disapproved of.

The Berlin reply swiftly ran into trouble. Huntington-Whiteley proved to be a quicker bowler than most they had faced and he clean-bowled both openers, Bruno Behnke and Bernhard Dartsch (Bruno's brother), for 4 and 0 respectively, while Deeley's medium pace accounted for Mader and Bruno Dartsch for single figures. By now the Major had realized that few of the German batsmen possessed the strength or technique to hit over the infield, so he brought his ring of fielders in to save the single. By drying up the runs he forced them to try and hit over the top when he came on to bowl his slow left-armers. The plan worked: the Berliners tried to slog their way out of trouble and succeeded only in being caught in the infield. The Major claimed four wickets as the hosts slumped to 62 all out, only Dietz reaching double figures. He joint top-scored on 17 with extras.

In the Gents' second innings Peter Terry opened with Dickie Williams.* Both fell cheaply to the willing Thamer before Captain Berkeley and Robin Whetherly took the

---

* Why the teams chose to play a four-innings match in one day is unclear. In Germany, as in England, it was common to play single-innings matches over one day and four innings over two days. Perhaps it was an attempt to give the Gents as much opportunity as possible to acclimatize. Or was it agreed in anticipation of a low-scoring match?

game away from the Berliners with a half-century stand. Whetherly smashed 57, including three huge sixes that cleared the clubhouse and drew gasps of astonishment from the crowd, while Berkeley stroked his way to an unbeaten 37 before the Major declared with the Gents 118 for 3. This left the Germans an improbable 204 to win in what remained of the day's play.

Their second innings followed the same pattern as the first: the top order failed and no one was capable of coping with the flight and guile of the Major's bowling. He took three wickets this time, supplemented by three from Charles Anton's medium pace and whatever it was that Williams bowled – history has not recorded that. The Major had only brought him on to gift the Germans a few easy runs to boost both the total and their confidence. The plan backfired when Williams took two wickets in his first over and had to be taken off. The home side's only consolation was that two men were able to reach double figures rather than one: Paul Gruhn of the Kickers club, who was also a tennis coach, and, most heartening of all, Rolf Zickert, one of the youngest players in the German squad, which at least augured well for the future. But their final total of 72 meant a victory for the Gents of somewhere between 131 and 101 runs, depending on the scorecard. The specifics aside, the tourists had managed to recover from a precarious start to achieve a resounding victory.

Plum Warner would be a happy man. But this was merely a warm-up against an average Berlin side. The real challenge, the tourists believed, would come the next day.

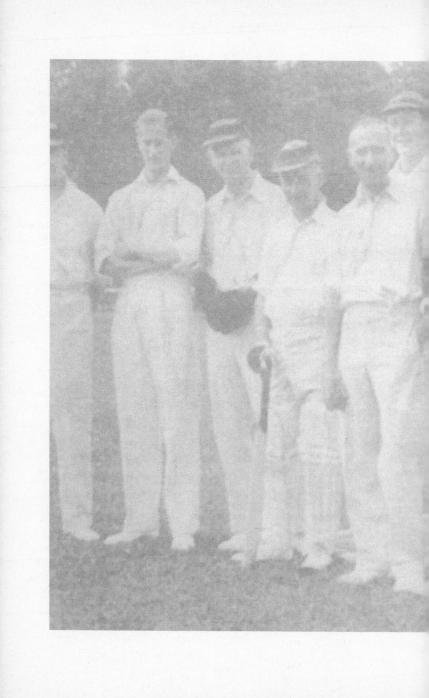

9

THE FIRST 'TEST'

BERLIN'S MORNING newspapers offered an honest judgement of the opening match of the tour: the hosts had lost to a far better side. There was praise for both the Gents' performance and, curiously, their physique: 'The English, all of them tall and sinewy in appearance, a team comprised of old and young players, reigned over this match from the very beginning.' *Volkische Beobachter* claimed that 147 was the highest innings score in Germany. This wasn't true – Dartford had scored 202 for 4 in their second innings on the same ground in 1931, though it was the only three-figure score they mustered throughout their four-match tour. 'The British batsmen were up first,' the newspaper gushed. 'They were not shy to show off their skills. A wonderful technical defence of the wickets and excellent batting soon resulted in a record number of runs of 147 in the first innings . . . Once it was the Berlin team's turn to bat, they were opposed by the impeccable skills of the guest team in the field. The bowling was beautiful, the tactical positioning in the field most impressive and therefore, the English team only permitted the German 62 runs.'

The Berliners may have been bloodied but they were not yet bowed. The same newspaper vowed the second match would be a better contest because their best players would be on the field: 'The team of Gau III which will play today at 11.30 a.m. and on Sunday at 11.30 a.m. on the Tib field in Hasenheide will be stronger. This means that the match should be more exciting than the first meeting.' And as a two-day match it would also therefore be an unofficial 'Test'.

The Germans intended to replace almost the entire eleven for this second match. The teams announced on the morning of the 6th in *Das Fußball-Megaphon* had Gerhard Thamer captaining the seconds and Felix Menzel skippering the stronger side; only Mader, Bernhard Dartsch and the home squad's best fielder Kuno Lehmann were picked for both matches. But on the morning of the 7th it was announced that Thamer would play *and* captain. His selection was difficult to argue with – he had taken seven wickets the day before and been one of his side's few successes – but it's difficult to see his appointment as captain ahead of Menzel as anything other than a politically motivated decision. Whatever his connections, Felix Menzel was not a Nazi. According to members of the Gents, Thamer was a fully fledged Nazi; there was even a suggestion he was an instructor in the Hitler Youth movement. He was a more palatable choice for the powers-that-be in such a high-profile encounter. Even though he was slightly built, he was strident, aggressive and vociferous – traits unlikely to endear him to the Gents. The Major started referring to him, out of earshot, as the 'Reichsportskaptain', and not as a mark of respect.

Together with the veteran Menzel brothers and the stalwart keeper Alfred Ladwig, the Berlin 1st XI featured some of the next generation of German cricketers. Gustav Parnemann was a talented football player who had been released early from a training camp for the Student Football World Championship, though he was recovering from a fractured nose. Egon Maus was a free-scoring batsman and remains the only German cricketer to be immortalized in

English literature. In C. P. Snow's *The Light and the Dark*, gifted scholar Roy Calvert writes a postcard to his friend Lewis Eliot which reads: 'Berlin. The best cricketer of German nationality is Maus (All German cricketers appear to have very short names). He is slightly worse than I am, slightly better than you.'* And there was insurance agent Kurt Rietz, perhaps the finest batsman in Berlin and a man who, like Felix Menzel, was consumed by a passion for the sport. At thirty-two he was already a fixture of the Berlin cricket scene, even though cricket at his normal club Viktoria 89 had ceased (he played for Amateure instead). *Das Fußball-Megaphon* highlighted his all-round capabilities, describing him as 'an extraordinary bowler. On a good day, he is also an excellent batsman.'

Regardless of what the press claimed, however, the Berlin team was not the strongest the city could offer. It was missing its best player, probably the country's finest home-grown cricketer of the twentieth century: Arthur Schmidt. He had been dangerous enough on turf wickets in England in 1930 where he had taken eight wickets with his looping left-arm spin, as well as finishing second in the batting averages; but on matting wickets he was lethal. During the Dartford tour of 1931, his thirty-two wickets in three matches at the astonishing average of 5.43 including fourteen victims in one match and three seven-wicket hauls. The only match he missed was

---

* The book was written in 1947. It's not clear how Snow, a Labour politician, chemist, civil servant and novelist, came across Maus's name.

the one in which Dartford scored that 202 for 4; their best innings score against a bowling attack with him in it was 96. With Felix Menzel he formed a formidable bowling partnership: Felix tied down the Dartford batsmen with his accurate seamers from one end while Schmidt's flight taunted and teased from the other. The Berliners drew the series 2–2. Had Schmidt and Felix played every match there's more than a good chance they would have won it. 'When they both could not play . . . it seemed like the English were the only team playing,' *FuWo* wrote after the tour was over. 'We missed their refined and powerful bowling – those two made Berlin proud.'

Schmidt's exploits won him publicity, even for a niche sport like cricket in Berlin. *FuWo* labelled him 'the Sobek of cricket' – a reference to Hanne Sobek, who played for Hertha Berlin and Germany between the wars and was regarded as the city's finest footballer. 'Glorious' was another word they used to describe his bowling against Dartford.

So where was he in 1937? Umpiring, is the answer. He and Georg Schneider were appointed *Schiedsrichter* for all three matches. Was he carrying an injury? Unlikely – Alfred Ladwig was missing half his feet but he still played. Schmidt was overweight – had he simply got too fat? As he bowled left-arm spin off a run-up of only a few paces and dealt in boundaries rather than ones or twos when he batted, that also seems an unlikely reason for his absence from the team; as we know, cricket is forgiving to the rotund male. Was he too old, then? It's true that a British newspaper referred to him as being in the 'veteran stage' during the 1930 tour. But they included Ladwig and Guido Menzel in that description and both were still playing in 1937. Felix was also in his mid forties, and the opposition featured several men who were advancing into middle age. This was a wonderful opportunity for Schmidt to pit his wits against a fine group of cricketers, including some who had played first-class cricket. Even if he had retired, surely he would have dusted off his whites and returned for a final bow? It's hard to imagine a man of his talents would be content to stand behind the stumps and watch inferior men play instead.

There is another, more sinister explanation. Schmidt was known by the nickname 'Mauschel'. Even the local press used it in their reports. The word had several meanings and its exact definition is difficult to pin down, but predominantly in Germany in the 1930s it was used to refer to someone who was Jewish. It was often derogatory, but it could also be used with a twinkle in one's eye to describe someone who has secret dealings, or is willing to cheat and schmooze to get his own way. If it was the latter, there is a chance Schmidt was not Jewish; he merely acted 'Jewish', in a manner or with a method that earned the sobriquet. But given the nickname *and* his bewildering exclusion from the side in 1937, there is more than a good chance he was Jewish.

If he was Jewish he had no hope of being allowed to play. Hitler had launched his cultural war against the Jews in 1933 and subsequently arrogated a series of powers to secure his position and destroy any meaningful opposition for good. An Enabling Act permitted the SA and the Gestapo to arrest anyone they pleased and detain them without charge. The Act was passed on a Friday; by the following Monday these powers were being used to terrorize and intimidate the Jews of Germany. It was decreed that all Jewish businesses should be boycotted and all 'Aryan' businesses should fire their

Jewish employees. As the summer progressed, Jews were dismissed from the Civil Service, Jewish doctors fired from hospitals, Jewish professors released from universities, and Jewish businesses forced to close.

On 2 June 1933 the Nazis officially ordered the expulsion of Jews from welfare organizations, youth clubs and sporting clubs and associations.* Nazi spokesman Bruno Malitz, in a letter which was sent to every sports club in Germany, condemned modern sports because they were 'infested with Frenchmen, Belgians, Pollacks and Jew-Niggers'. The virulently racist mouthpiece of the Nazi regime, *Der Sturmer*, made the point crystal clear: 'Jews are Jews and there is no place for them in German sports.' By the end of 1933 Jews were banned from every tennis, boxing, gymnastics and rowing club; shortly afterwards they were barred even from swimming in public baths. This was all part of Hitler and the Nazis' policy of *Gleichschaltung* ('forcing into line'), which compelled club members to prove they were of Aryan descent, insisted that all young members join the Hitler Youth, and appointed party place-men in senior positions at every sports association.

Football, the most popular sport, was no exception. Even before the decree ordering expulsion, in a pathetic attempt to curry favour with their new masters the Deutsche Fussball Bund (DFB) had announced that Jews and Marxists were 'deemed unacceptable'. The DFB's press officer Guido von Mengden would later state that 'National Socialism has

---

* Guy Walters, in his book about the 1936 Berlin Olympics, points out that the Nazis tried to pretend they had never issued such a decree. But it was a blatant lie.

restored the meaning of sport', adding the observation that 'footballers are political soldiers of the Führer'. There is no reason to believe cricket was any different.

But if Schmidt was Jewish, given that background he would have been prevented even from umpiring. However, in the run-up to the 1936 Olympics, to appease international opinion, the Nazis had allowed German Jews to compete in the Games. One year on and that amnesty was forgotten – Jews were once again suffering horrendous persecution – but the arrival of an English team put everyone on their best behaviour. There was no way Schmidt would be allowed to play, but it's feasible he might have been allowed to umpire. The Berliners were short of qualified men to do the job, and the last thing the Nazis wanted was to embarrass their guests with poor officiating. Schmidt was experienced, he knew the rules, and he had the respect of the Berlin team, as a cricketer at least. Who knows, perhaps Felix Menzel asked for him personally. It's a possibility that only one of Schmidt's grandparents had been Jewish, therefore he was more likely to escape persecution – for the time being. Or he might have been married to an Aryan woman, which could have shielded him from the worst excesses of the anti-Jewish ordinances. Whatever the explanation, his expertise almost certainly meant it was worth allowing him to stand.

The first 'Test' was held at the Turngemeinde in Berlin (TiB) sports club beside the Hasenheide Park, across the road from Tempelhof Airport. This time the Gents' taxis took them down the entire length of Wilhelmstrasse, past the Gestapo headquarters where countless men and women were tortured and interrogated in basement cells, and the building where the appalling Reinhard Heydrich coordinated and planned some of the worst atrocities of the Nazi era. Heydrich is rightly regarded as the most sadistic figure in the Nazi elite; even Hitler described him as 'The Man with the Iron Heart'.

The Reich Security HQ wasn't the only Nazi house of horror the Gents passed on their way to that morning's match. As they turned left on to Columbiadamm they passed the site of the recently closed Columbia concentration camp where thousands of communists, social democrats, Jews and other opponents of the regime had been detained and tortured. It was in this camp, one of the first of its kind when it was opened in 1933, that many of the architects of the Holocaust learned their grim trade. It had closed nine months before the Gents arrived and the nearby airport had swallowed its buildings. There were still 150 other detention camps in and around the city, though.

The TiB ground was and remains one of the most picturesque sports grounds in Berlin. A gym and tennis club, it's located only a few metres from where the German 'Turnvater' Friedrich Ludwig Jahn started the first open-air gymnasium (*Turnplatz*) in the city, in 1811, thirty-seven years before the TiB club was formed. The match with the Gents appears to be the first and only cricket game to be played there, which shows how keen the organizers were to impress their visitors – though, however scenic their surroundings, they were still playing on the same stretch of matting as the day before.

Cyril Smith was still unwell so Peter Robinson was

included in the Gents side again and they were given first use of the pitch for the second game running. Even though it was a Saturday the crowd was disappointing, perhaps discouraged by the result of the first match. Young Maurice Jewell was later to say enigmatically that among the spectators 'were some rather lovely ladies – too old for me but, perhaps, the seniors had made their acquaintance'. Which begs the question where had the older Gents met them? Both William Deeley and Dickie Williams were bachelors; perhaps they had done the acquainting. The Gents had a history of scoring off the pitch as well as on it: Cyril Smith had met his future wife during their tour of Portugal.

Whether it was the pleasant surroundings, a flatter, better-kept field to play on, the experience of playing on matting the previous day, or even the attentions of some attractive women in the crowd, the Gents' batting was far sturdier on that first morning. Felix and Guido Menzel opened the bowling and immediately impressed; like the day before, the German fielders were arranged in a ring on the leg side and the brothers bowled short of a good length on leg stump. The Major fell into the trap and was caught by Maus for a single with just three runs on the board, but Williams and Terry, hitherto struggling for runs, found a method to survive and score. Terry made 22 before he was bowled, and when Guido trapped Williams lbw for 40 there was a flurry of wickets: Berkeley, Whetherly and Young Maurice all fell to Felix and there was a chance, for the second day in succession, for the Berliners to dismiss the Englishmen cheaply. But their deep batting line-up proved to be their saviour once more. This time it was Deeley who changed their fortunes with a 64, ably assisted by Geoffrey Tomkinson's half century.

William Deeley was forty-four but in excellent shape; lantern-jawed, grey-haired and distinguished. A grammar school pupil, he was the team's self-made man – as shown by his lack of initials: he was simply W. Deeley, as if he was the team's pro. He'd left school to become clerk to a stockbroker in Birmingham before becoming a broker himself, and a successful one too if the time he took off to play cricket in the twenties and thirties is any indication. As well as the Gents he played games for Fosseway House, a country house team the Major also played for, and the famous nomadic Free Foresters. He lived alone in Alvechurch and became a mainstay of Barnt Green Cricket Club, now one of the strongest teams in the Birmingham League, where Deeley is still fondly remembered as a kindly, classy gentleman of the old school – immaculately turned out and effortlessly charming with a gentle, dry sense of humour. Unlike other former players* he was never the sort to moan about the state of the modern game or to reminisce about better days.

When he and Tomkinson were finally dismissed, Peter Huntington-Whiteley smashed an ebullient 36 while Peter Robinson kept his end up with a gutsy 2. Their partnership and the Gents innings were to end in controversial circumstances. As Robinson backed up at the non-striker's end, the unnamed bowler ran him out. 'He never warned me!' Robinson would write later. The Germans seemed to be unaware they had transgressed one of the game's great taboos. Robinson was obviously shocked, a

---

* G. S. Tomkinson for one. He became renowned for spouting off about slow-scoring post-war cricket. He blamed slow pitches for blunting the strokes of batsmen.

feeling shared among his teammates. But it was down to the captain to reverse the appeal and ask the batsman back and it's obvious that either Gerhard Thamer wasn't one for such diplomacy or he simply wasn't aware of the correct cricketing etiquette.

Despite this unedifying end to their innings the Gents were satisfied with their total of 271, which definitely *was* a record score for Germany. The Gents players and the crowd gave Felix Menzel a resounding ovation as he left the field having taken seven of the ten wickets to fall. Without him the score could have been much higher, and it was only the blazing summer heat which forced him off after his opening spell and allowed the stand between Deeley and Tomkinson to prosper. It had been a remarkable effort that won the respect of his opponents.

The reply was a disaster for the Germans: they were bowled out for 48. The scorecard for this innings has been lost but *FuWo*'s correspondent wrote a detailed report of the carnage. 'Even though expectations weren't very high, the resulting score of 48 runs against 271 left much to be desired. Three men did not score at all! Only the two Preußen players Parnemann and Maus were able to bat 12 and 9 runs. The guests played an amazing game, putting their incredible fielding skills to good use they made sure that the men of Gau III did not spend a long time at the wickets.' The same correspondent singled out Deeley and Huntington-Whiteley as the finest bowlers, so it is safe to assume they took most of the wickets. Huntington-Whiteley took three wickets in a ten-minute spell and his pace amazed the spectators. 'We did not know that cricket balls could be played with such sharpness and force and could be thrown with an arm as widely extended,' the correspondent added. He was also impressed with Whetherly's 'extraordinary' glovework. 'This agile 21-year-old caught the fastest balls with incredible precision, reacted at lightning speed and pushed out as soon as the team from Berlin got careless.' Which would indicate that some of the Berlin players were out stumped.

The Gents shrugged off any temptation to enforce the follow-on out of fear it might seem like bullying and went back out to bat before the close of play. Peter Huntington-Whiteley, given a rare chance to open, and Peter Terry were both victims of Guido Menzel for 2 and 6 respectively but at stumps Dickie Williams and Captain Berkeley were unbeaten and the lead was a whopping 285.

That evening the young Gents – the three Peters and Young Maurice – ate at a small inn just off the Unter den Linden. Probably owing to the strong position their side was in, they felt the need to celebrate. After their meal they decided to have a ten-pfennig cigar each, though Robinson changed his mind and had three cigarettes instead. 'I shall not have any more, because I don't think they are especially appetising,' he promised his mum and dad in a letter. Reading his letters when they finally reached England, poor Mrs Robinson could be forgiven for wondering what had become of her darling son: in only four days away from home he had drunk beer for breakfast, visited one of Berlin's most notorious fleshpots and tried smoking.

That evening's after-dinner entertainment was more wholesome: a trip to the movies to see *Lloyd's of London* starring Tyrone Power and Madeleine Carroll, which managed the not inconsiderable feat of being a huge box-office success even though its theme was the birth of the insurance industry. Hitler was a movie buff, often watching films late into the night, and the Nazis knew that American films were popular and a boost to the economy as long as their messages didn't clash with their own philosophy. *Lloyd's of London*'s plot about financial acumen underpinning military might – in this case the British Navy against the dastardly Napoleon – ticked all the appropriate boxes.

The supporting cast included C. Aubrey Smith, possessor of the finest moustache in cinema history. Smith was also a fanatical cricketer who played for Sussex in the late nineteenth century. He played one Test match, too, as captain, and took 5 for 19. In 1932 he set up the Hollywood Cricket Club in Los Angeles and persuaded David Niven, Errol Flynn, Laurence Olivier and Boris Karloff to play. Smith was also the source of some of cricket's finest anecdotes. One involves him being asked to field at slip for Hollywood, at which point he asked his butler to bring out his glasses. After he put them on, a ball looped to him at slip, a dolly 'a child could take at midnight with no moon' according to one present. Smith dropped it and took off his spectacles to examine them. 'Damn fool brought my reading glasses,' he harrumphed. Another anecdote highlights the somewhat narrow interests of the average MCC member. Smith was back in the country, basking in the box-office success of *The Prisoner of Zenda* and enjoying a match in the Lord's Pavilion. 'I say, that chap over there does look awfully familiar,' one member is reported to have told another, spying Smith's distinctive features and impressive whiskers. 'Yes,' came the reply. 'Chap called Smith. Used to play for Sussex.'

The Gents retired to their hotel tired but happy; they had struck a decisive blow on the first day of the first important match of the tour. Felix Menzel and his side were less satisfied. Their only hope of saving the game was to *beten für Regen* – pray for rain.

10

'A VERY RELAXING SPORT'

BY THEIR FIFTH day in Berlin, Peter Robinson and Peter Terry had developed a routine. Play did not start until 11.30 and to avoid having to get up early the two boys had started having breakfast in bed. As he lounged in his on the morning of the 8th, Robinson wrote another letter to his mother in which he voiced doubts about whether he would play in the third and last match of the tour because Cyril Smith appeared to be recovering from his illness. He also confessed that he had spent forty-five Deutschmarks, mainly on taxis to and from the ground. Then he realized it was 9.30 a.m. – 'I suppose I must get up!'

Back at the TiB-Platz, the sun was as merciless as the Gents batsmen – thirty degrees and not a cloud in the sky. Gerhard Thamer put himself on and almost immediately accounted for Captain Berkeley for 28; he followed this by trapping Whetherly lbw for a duck.* The Berliners were proving once again that they would not submit meekly. But their fightback ended when the Major joined Dickie Williams and the pair built a half-century stand. When the Major fell for 29, William Deeley came in and carried on where his captain left off.

Williams completed his fifty and continued to nudge his way towards the first hundred ever scored on German soil.

* Another scorecard claims that Peter Robinson was sent in after Whetherly and was also out for a duck, but not the one printed in *The Cricketer*.

It's unlikely to have made exciting viewing. Williams was a shy, retiring character who ran a glove factory and lived in Stourbridge with his two sisters Dolly and Daisy (therefore filling the role of Private Godfrey in our cricketing prequel of *Dad's Army*). His batting reflected his character, cautious and workmanlike; he was 'a dogged accumulator of runs' according to his nephew. In a team of Cavaliers he was very much a Roundhead who brandished the broadsword rather than the rapier.

As a young man he had been good enough to earn a few matches for Worcestershire, where he became known to the Major, but he was not talented enough to make any sort of impression at that level. Over the course of thirty-seven matches and nine painfully mediocre years he only passed fifty twice, and one of those came in a dead match against Nottinghamshire when the opposing captain bowled his part-timers rather than Harold Larwood and Bill Voce. Like Geoffrey Tomkinson, he compensated for a lack of first-class success by scoring heavily in league cricket for Stourbridge. Few club records of that era have survived, but there is one old scorebook which records a match between Stourbridge and Old Hill in 1926. Old Hill had a new pro, a miner called Aaron Lockett whose 'fast off-spin' was often unplayable. As it proved that day: at one stage he had taken seven wickets for no runs, and he ended up with 10 for 14 as Stourbridge were bowled out for 26. Dickie Williams opened that day and carried his bat – for 0 not out! A heroic piece of resistance to gladden the heart of dour stonewallers everywhere.

According to Keith Jones, a Stourbridge member of long standing, one summer's day in 1978 Dickie returned to Stourbridge CC for the fiftieth anniversary ceremony for the pavilion. A member of the club committee passed him the scorebook with the gruesome details of that match against Old Hill fifty-two years earlier. Dickie, aged seventy-four, handed it straight back with barely concealed disgust. 'He chucked it anyway,' he said, referring to Lockett.*

Williams completed his hundred and so carved a legend of his own – the first man to score a century in Germany. Perhaps it was watching him nudge and nurdle his way to this painstaking ton that prompted the man from *Die Fußball-Woche* to ruffle a few feathers by declaring that he found the breaks for lunch and tea the most entertaining parts of the game. 'For a Cricket specialist this is, of course, blasphemy – but we were only joking! In fact breaks are something lovely and part of Cricket. In England during breaks the players and spectators come together for a relaxing "tea". Cricket is, even though competitive, a very relaxing sport,' he backtracked diplomatically.

Guido Menzel eventually bowled Williams for 104 and the Gents' innings ended shortly afterwards: they had scored 240, an overall lead of 463. The Berliners walked out to the middle knowing that victory was impossible but hoping to bat for a draw, or at the very least salvage some pride. They began well enough: Egon Maus and Gustav Parnemann put together their first double-figure opening partnership of

---

* Aaron Lockett is of a breed the leagues know only too well: players who should have played first-class cricket but instead chose to carve their name into league legend. Not only was his bowling lethal in the right conditions, he could bat too. In 1928 he scored 154 for the Minor Counties against a touring West Indies team that featured Sir Learie Constantine. Lockett played until he was sixty-nine and was so dedicated to the game that in winter he converted his garden path into a concrete wicket to practise on.

the series until the latter was bowled by C. S. Anton, who would become the latest of the Gents old guard to make a significant contribution. Parnemann's dismissal led to the inevitable collapse: Mader, Bernhard Dartsch, Kurt Rietz, Zehmke, Guido Menzel and Gerhard Thamer all fell in quick succession. Maus resisted stoically, having learned the art of patience from watching Williams, spending more than an hour compiling his 35 until he became Anton's fifth wicket, all bowled. By now the correspondent of *Die Fußball-Woche* was paying enough attention to note how the Gents had employed the same tactic of moving closer in to stop Maus from scoring from his glances and cut shots, forcing him to try and hit over the top.

The end couldn't come soon enough for the Gents, who were struggling in the heat. Maus was only able to resist for so long because Peter Huntington-Whiteley, who had decimated the top order the day before, was too ill to bowl. Young Maurice had to leave the field for a short time too, and Peter Robinson wrote that he felt 'absolutely rotten'. Were the cigars and cigarettes of the night before at fault? Peter didn't think so. 'I think it was a touch of the sun mingled with a bilious attack from the greasy food we get here,' he told his younger brother in a letter. Charles Anton also complained of being unwell, which makes his five-wicket haul even more impressive.

Felix Menzel and Alfred Ladwig launched a brave if futile counter-attack. Fips was especially severe on the Major in scoring 26; he landed some lusty blows before Maurice finally got his man. Meanwhile Ladwig helped himself to 32 in a stubborn last-wicket stand with Bruno Dartsch, whom the Gents had permitted to play and bat as a substitute for the injured Kuno Lehmann. As the shadows lengthened across the Hasenheide, Dickie Williams bowled Dartsch to end the match. The *FuWo* correspondent was relieved the home side had shown some fight:

> Fips Menzel with his gutsy attitude batted 26 runs and to everyone's surprise, the two last men, Dartsch II and Ladwig, were so successful, that they increased the running score of the Berlin team from 104 to 150! This was more than we could hope for. The Berlin team played an excellent game. You have to remember that they are playing their game under difficult circumstances. For decades it is more or less the same players who play this game, so the expectations in the team are not very high and there is no competition to spur them on – one has to pay our Cricketers their respect! They can be very proud of their skills in this rather unknown sport.

Overall, despite another resounding defeat, the correspondent felt the cause of cricket in Germany had been furthered, though he then went on to list the reasons why the sport might never catch the German sporting public's imagination.

> The 'Gentlemen of Worcestershire' showcased their sport in a beautiful, impressing manner which not only showed the competitive side of the sport but was at the same time an interesting lesson in the art of Cricket! The Cricketers from Berlin had to acknowledge their inferiority but they proved to be intent and observant students. If Cricket will indeed gain support from central forces, just as

the fans from Berlin hope it will, then one day at least a small part of their dream will become true. There are some basic difficulties which prevent the expansion of the sport in Germany. It is less external factors but rather the difficulties stemming from the difference in national characters, the difference between English and German temperaments. It is a great thing to strive for this 'poised serenity' which is the basic element of a magnificent mind – in England this is part of daily life, they have the expression 'It's Cricket!' – but for Germans it is very hard to achieve this laudable skill! Or at least the English have a clear advantage over the Germans when it comes to striv[ing] for mental balance.

Monday, 9 August presented the Gents with their last off day of the tour, a chance to rest stiff and weary limbs and explore more of the city's sights. In its tour preview, *Das Fußball-Megaphon* informed its readers the tourists would spend their spare days visiting Schloss Sanssouci in Potsdam and a 'Reich's Labour Service Camp'. These camps had originally been set up in the Weimar period to alleviate the effects of high unemployment but under Hitler and the Nazis had become a six-month compulsory service that prepared men and women for the Army and ultimately war; their main purpose was to indoctrinate young men and women in Nazi ideology. For reasons unknown the trip was cancelled. It's unlikely that the Gents were too disappointed.

The trip to Sanssouci Palace went ahead, however. The Reichssportführer laid on official cars with drivers, each vehicle flying the Nazi flag of an eagle perched on top of a swastika. According to Young Maurice Jewell, when the cars approached a junction they sounded their 'special' horns and the police stopped all traffic so they could pass without hindrance. The police believed the cars were carrying high-ranking party dignitaries rather than a group of English cricketers and offered the Nazi salute.

Despite their eagerness to be courteous guests, some of the Gents were starting to feel a nagging disquiet. This wasn't caused by events on the field – though the Berliners' constant appealing and disregard for the delicacies of the game had been unnerving – but their experiences off it. For a start there were the everyday aspects of Berlin life at that time: SS men patrolling the street, buildings festooned with Nazi flags, anti-Semitic signs proclaiming 'Jews Unwelcome', all of which made them uneasy. We know Robin Whetherly was able to speak and read German and he may well have translated for his teammates. Even more alarmingly, according to Young Maurice, 'Wherever we played, we could hear machine-guns firing.' The senior Gents – Peter Robinson's letters don't hint at any consternation at all – sensed something was 'odd' and that Nazi Germany was a 'strange country'.

It must have been a relief, therefore, to escape the city for a few hours to visit the former summer palace of the Prussian king Frederick the Great, in a time when the region was run by enlightened absolutists and not absolute nihilists. There were terraced gardens galore for Captain Berkeley to inspect, not to mention the three thousand fruit trees, greenhouses and nurseries laid out in the adjoining park. Inside the palace the Gents were able to admire its marble halls, rococo design, galleries and circular library.

Berlin was in the grip of a heatwave so the cars took those who wanted to swim from Potsdam to Wannsee (Peter Robinson had been hoping to swim in the Olympic pool at the Olympiastadion and had bought a new pair of trunks especially, but it appears permission was denied). The Strandbad Wannsee was an open-air lido, phenomenally popular with Berliners looking to escape the choking heat of summer in the city. It was also the site of a popular nudist beach, though there is no confirmation the Gents visited that area. Nor would they have seen signs prohibiting Jews from using the lido – they had been taken down ahead of the 1936 Olympics and would not reappear until 1938.

Wannsee had always been a place where people met and talked and had occasionally been the scene of political fights and scuffles between rival groups. The Nazis' paranoia and lust for control meant they were unwilling to tolerate the idea of people gathering and chatting without scrutiny. Even something as simple as going for a swim or lying in the sun while the children played on the beach needed to be monitored. So they'd seized control of the entire complex and appointed party officials to run it. Its managing director since 1924 had been Hermann Clajus, a large, jovial man. The lido was his life: it had been built to his specifications and he had watched with enormous pride as it became a central part of Berlin culture. But he was a trade unionist and social democrat, which to Nazi eyes made him a dangerous traitor. There was no chance he would be allowed to hold a position of responsibility. In March 1933 he learned that he was to be replaced as manager and that it was likely he would be arrested. Rather than face that ignominy, he killed himself. Tragedies such as this were a daily occurrence in

Nazi Germany: men and women would rather commit suicide than submit to Nazi brutality and watch as their lives were ruined.

This mania for spying on their own citizens extended to tourists and visitors, including the Worcester Gents. According to Charles Anton, wherever the team went, whether to a restaurant for a meal or the beach for a swim, even for a simple walk to the shops, they were watched 'rather carefully'. A close eye was kept on them during their matches, presumably from the crowd, unless Thamer or one of the other players was tasked with finding out whether the Gents were up to anything secretive in the middle.

Sunned and relaxed, the team returned to the Adlon where they received some bad news: Cyril Smith's illness had deteriorated and he had been rushed to hospital. The eventual diagnosis was pneumonia. For a few hours his life was in grave danger. He'd only survived because a doctor at the hospital insisted on an X-ray, which showed the presence of disease on both lungs and allowed them to begin treatment immediately. A few more hours without treatment and he would have died.

That evening the Gents returned to Haus Vaterland, though this time the junior members of the side were granted less freedom. 'We came back after a very short time,' Peter Robinson wrote, 'as Major Jewell advised an early bed, in spite of the fact that I slept from 10.30 p.m. to 9.30 a.m. the night before.' Perhaps the Major didn't want anyone else to fall ill, or he was aware of how some of the younger members of the team had struggled to cope with the hot weather the day before and didn't want them to burn the candle at both ends. Smith's illness meant that Robinson would be playing the next day, which would give him the chance to improve on his abysmal form. His fielding had offered some consolation: 'On Sunday . . . I caught a very good catch at 2nd slip but I missed a very hard one at close-in gully. The batsman could have knocked my head off where I was.'

When he, the other two Peters and Maurice Jewell returned to their rooms that night they discovered an envelope had been slipped under their doors. It was stamped with the eagle and swastika symbol and the address of the Deutsche Reichsbund für Leibesübungen, Fachamt Fussball (Football Office). It was an official invitation from the Ministry of Sport. (On both the envelope and in the letter itself, Robinson's name had been handwritten and Michael Mallinson's scratched out – an indication of how late his inclusion in the party was.)

Date: 9. August 1937

To celebrate the presence of the English Cricket team 'The Gentlemen of Worcestershire' the Reichsfachamtsleiter had initially invited you to the Hotel 'Russischer Hof' on the 11. August 1937.

Please note that the location has changed and the event will now take place on Wednesday, the 11. August at 8 pm in the Stadion-Terrassen of the Reichssportfeld station.

Reichsfachamt Football, Rugby, Cricket
Head: Signature (on behalf of) Hörbrand

After perusing the letter, they got their heads down. The next day's match was the crowning moment of the tour – a chance to play at the prestigious Olympiastadion.

11

THE HOUSE OF
GERMAN SPORT

O N THEIR FIRST day in Berlin the Gents had visited the Olympiastadion, silent and stately in the summer sun rather than the cauldron of baying fanaticism it had been the year before. The sheer scale of the stadium took the team's breath away. At the time there was nothing like it in the world. A limestone amphitheatre sunk forty feet below sea level so that the exterior didn't give a hint of the vastness within, it was capable of holding a hundred thousand spectators. The Gents toured the stadium and walked the track where Jesse Owens had won gold before crossing the vast Maifeld to climb the 247-foot bell tower and view the colossal 30,000lb bell which had tolled to summon spectators and participants to the Olympic Games.

If that filled them with a sense of awe and admiration, their tour of the Langemarckhalle beneath the bell tower created a sense of unease. The hall had been built to honour the German dead who fell at the Battle of Langemarck in Flanders in 1914. In *Mein Kampf* Hitler recounted the story of soldiers, all reservists or students straight from school, advancing on the enemy singing 'Deutschland, Deutschland Über Alles' as bullets and shellfire burst around them. It was pure myth: there were no songs and little glory, just the usual senseless slaughter. But in Hitler's narrative they were transformed into martyrs – the flower of German youth who had laid down their lives for the glory of their country only to have their memory betrayed by the surrender of their cowardly, craven leaders. Carved on the wall were some words from a poem by Friedrich Hölderlin about the 'fallen':

> Live above, O Fatherland,
> And don't count the dead.
> For you, dear,
> Not a single man has fallen in vain.

The Nazis believed that sporting and military spirit were symbolically linked. Sacrifice on the field of play was a preparation for sacrifice in battle. But the Gents thought a sports stadium a curious place to erect such a shrine. Many of them had witnessed and survived the horrors of the First World War and believed in more sober tributes.

On 10 August they returned to the Olympiastadion to play the final match of their tour. It had originally been scheduled for the Maifeld, but was moved. The reasons aren't clear, but as the city was about to celebrate its seven hundredth anniversary it's likely the field was needed as a rehearsal ground for parades, processions and military drills. The match was moved to Schenkendorfplatz, one of several grounds that made up the German sports forum within the Olympic site. These grounds and fields surrounded the Haus des Deutschen Sports, which hosted the fencing events in the Olympics and then became the offices of the Reichssportführer and his ministry. From the pitch, the Gents would have been able to see the two large columns that stand outside its main entrance, crowned once again by the ubiquitous gold eagles and swastikas. The two previous matches had been played on sports grounds that were owned by the state, like all sport facilities, but which had retained their own character. The only evidence of Nazi control had been swastika flags fluttering from the clubhouses. Here there was no doubt. If the old trees, pergolas and tennis courts of Hasenheide Park had proved an idyllic backdrop to the second match, the columns, statues, memorials to the war dead and the vast stadium here were designed to strike awe into the hearts and minds of onlookers. It was the state's ideology written in stone.

Cyril Smith was still in hospital and his illness threatened to cast a pall over the final few days of the tour. Captain Berkeley was also absent. It's possible he was keeping Smith company in hospital, or it could have been that he had found a new garden to inspect. Whatever the reason, to prevent the Gents taking the field with ten men they were given Kuno Lehmann. The son of Fritz Lehmann, who had been one of the leading figures in German cricket before the Nazis came to power, Kuno had proved the best fielder in the Berlin side and the safest pair of hands. He was also a keen student of the game and a budding writer. In 1931 he had penned a piece ahead of the tour by Dartford CC in which he tried to interpret the rules of the MCC for budding umpires.

Given the thirty-degree weather the Major was glad of another pair of youthful legs, though, as in the previous two matches, the Gents batted first. The lush uncut grass on the Schenkendorfplatz outfield and its sheer size meant that boundaries would be hard to come by. That didn't stop the Major opening with Dickie Williams and it didn't prevent them putting on a half century as the German fielding wilted as quickly as their spirit. Once the openers had seen off the Menzel brothers, runs came easy and tempers started to fray in the Berlin side. The Major attempted a lofted drive off a seaming Gerhard Thamer delivery but succeeded only in skying the ball to mid-off where the youngest player on the team dropped it. Thamer had spent the entire series castigating his players for misfields and screaming his frustration whenever a chance went begging, much to the Gents' amusement: they had come to dislike him immensely, a feeling shared by a number of Thamer's teammates. This time Thamer seethed in silence. In his next over the same young player dropped an identical chance. Surely Thamer would explode? Again he said nothing. He simply walked over to where the young player was staring sheepishly at the grass and knocked him to the floor with a right hook. Then he picked up the ball and prepared to bowl the next delivery as the poor fielder writhed on the ground. The game continued.

This story became the most famous one of the tour. It was told time and time again. George Chesterton, Peter Huntington-Whiteley's childhood friend, referred to it in his letter; Phil Mackie mentioned it to me in an email. However, it's likely that the incident happened in a Berlin League game and not in this match, even though Thamer was still the culprit. James Coldham spoke to four members of the team and they all said they were *told* about the incident, presumably by someone like Felix Menzel, rather than experienced it. In their version, Thamer's team, BSV 92, were a man short for a match and he refused to start unless they had eleven. They managed to recruit a passing youth, gave him some whites, and Thamer placed him on the boundary at long off, out of harm's way. But in the first over he dropped a skyer. When it happened again in Thamer's second over, he walked over and punched him on the chin.

Regardless of when it happened, the right hook was

used to highlight a genuine problem in Berlin cricket: the younger generation were reluctant to take up the sport because of the retributive justice handed out on the field if they made a mistake. In a report for *The Cricketer* once the tour was over, Captain Berkeley addressed this problem. 'The young German players in Germany require coaching and encouragement,' he wrote, 'and some of the rather drastic punishment that is on occasions meted out to them when catches are missed could, with advantage to the game, be discontinued. A dropped catch, after all, is a mistake which anyone would avoid if possible, and is never done on purpose!!'

Williams' and the Major's opening stand continued. By this time the Reichssportführer had arrived to watch a few hours' play before hosting a tea for the participants. Gottfried von Cramm was also in the crowd, though Tschammer und Osten was probably the last person he wanted to see so soon after his epic defeat to Don Budge. Alongside him was his protégé and German number two, Henner Henkel.

Felix Menzel bowled Williams shortly before lunch for 43, and in the next session also picked up Peter Terry for 17. Even though the Berlin team were being outclassed, Felix was the one bowler who was able to contain the Gents batsmen. Thamer collected the wickets of Whetherly and Young Maurice, Parnemann accounted for Deeley, and the Berlin team were once again back in it. Not for the first time, Geoffrey Tomkinson strode to the wicket to stop the rot. At the other end, perhaps inspired by the illustrious guests in the crowd, the Major was rolling back the years. He went past his fifty and managed to reach his century before tea. It was a remarkable achievement, not least of stamina: the slow outfield and long boundaries meant he scored only three fours and had to run most of his runs, in searing heat.

If he thought he might have a chance to rest during the tea-break he was mistaken. The Reichssportführer was hosting his reception for the players at the Reiterhaus, a building on the other side of the Olympic complex near the stables. After four hours of batting under a hot sun the Major had to take off his pads and walk the best part of a mile in order to sit in a stuffy room for an hour (not the usual twenty minutes), and then give a short speech about how grateful his team was for the opportunity to demonstrate the English national game to the German people. He also offered his heartfelt support to the Berlin team and German cricket in general.

According to Captain Berkeley's son and one of Peter Terry's sons, Joseph Goebbels, the notorious Nazi Minister for Propaganda, also attended the match that day. By their accounts, Goebbels asked the Gents to pose for a picture with him but they refused. Their unease at the atmosphere in Nazi Berlin, perhaps reinforced in private conversations with non-Nazis such as Felix Menzel, had reached the stage where they didn't wish to be seen endorsing the regime.

But there is no documentary evidence that Goebbels was at the match. There is no record of it in his exhaustive diaries, no mention of cricket, nor any reference to his presence in the newspapers that reported on the match and usually acted as Goebbels' mouthpiece (though there is an argument which suggests that if Goebbels was snubbed it's unlikely such a discourtesy would have been reported). It is interesting to note that even though Tschammer und Osten watched the match and hosted tea, there are no photographs of him either. Perhaps the Gents refused to have their photo taken with him, or engineered a situation where it became impossible, then over time the subject of the snubbing was changed from the Reichssportführer to Dr Goebbels.

Once tea was done and the players had trudged back across to the ground, the Major carried on where he'd left off. He was eventually out for 140, which meant that Dickie Williams' German record had lasted just forty-eight hours.* He was given a rousing ovation on his way off the field, though he was too exhausted to raise his bat. He headed straight to a deckchair where he promptly fell asleep, still wearing his pads and batting gloves.

The Menzel brothers whittled away the lower order, with Felix taking five wickets. Kuno Lehmann scored 13, more in one innings for the Gents than he had managed in two innings for the Berliners, before the side were all out for a princely 265. There was enough time in the fading light before the close of play for Huntington-Whiteley and Deeley to test out the Berlin top order. With the luxury of a high first-innings score, the Major attacked with four slips and a gully. The pressure paid off: Parnemann ran himself out for 2, while Maus nicked the Etonian behind for 4. In the last over of the day Rietz, who was having a torrid time with the bat, became Huntington-Whiteley's second victim, clean-bowled for 5, to leave the Germans perched precariously on 19 for 3 when stumps were drawn.

That evening the Major managed to shake off his fatigue and accompany his team to Haus Vaterland for a final time, though once they had bathed and dressed their departure

---

* The Major's record would stand until it was surpassed by Shakoor Ahmed in 1955.

from the Adlon was delayed. As dusk became night on the Unter den Linden, the traffic ceased and thousands of people gathered on either side of the street, scores deep. A murmur of excitement started to ripple through the crowd. Almost in unison they raised and extended their arms in the Hitler salute. The Gents, observing from a hotel window, looked west towards the State Opera House. A glowing river of light was approaching, accompanied by an underlying percussion of boot on stone. Soon the Gents were able to see that the river of light was a mass of flaming torches held by endless columns of uniformed soldiers, SA and SS officers. The procession was so long that it took nearly an hour to pass the Adlon and head across Pariser Platz towards the Brandenburg Gate, draped for the occasion with swastika flags. The entire event took place in almost total silence – 'alarming and eerie' according to Young Maurice Jewell.

This time there were no early curfews for the team. The tension in Berlin was tangible and the pleasures of their favourite nightspot offered welcome respite.

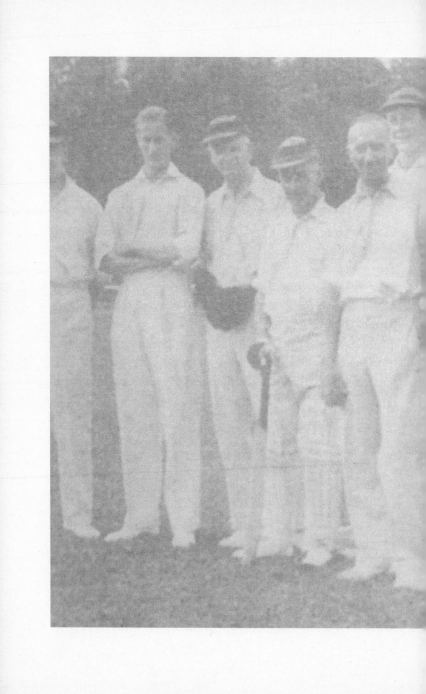

12

AUF WIEDERSEHEN, GOOD FELLOWS

THE SPORTS pages of the next day's newspapers, at least those that had not become disenchanted with the home team's performances and lost interest, were ablaze with praise for the Major's century. 'Major Jewell schlug Kricket-Rekord!' hailed the *Berliner-Zeitung. Reichssportblatt*, which as the state's official magazine was surely more used to admiring the form and fitness of lither, younger athletes than the Major, also hailed his achievement, though it got his age wrong (one wonders if a mischievous member of the Gents side deliberately fed the wrong information to wind up their very own Captain Mainwaring):

'Out! Out! Caught!' The small, chubby Berliner over there at the end of the cricket field shouted and threw his hat in the air and raised his hands in jubilation. The bowler shook out his tired arm to loosen it up again and the wicketkeeper behind the stumps mopped the sweat off his brow. What a piece of work this had been to get the English Major to leave the batting station. The old Jewell had struck one hundred and forty runs before he was dismissed. The fifty-five-year-old stopped brilliant throws and beat every ball that was thrown with spin on or near the stumps far out into the field, always in-between the players of the Berlin team.

They balanced their praise of age and experience with heart-felt appreciations of Huntington-Whiteley's bowling and Whetherly's keeping:

> When the formidable English man approached with the ball, arm extended far behind and threw the ball flat and sharp towards the stumps, the bails bounced on the stumps, and many members of the Berlin team had to leave the game prematurely. This proved to be a difficult situation for the batter, especially having five gentlemen on his batting side ready to catch each rebound or ball which wasn't stopped correctly. Add to this a wicketkeeper with an awe-inspiring ability for catching balls, an artistic flexibility and hands always ready to push – such were the skills of the English team member Wetherley [*sic*]!

When the players reconvened on Wednesday morning, any hopes that the Berliners would mount a stirring come-back were swiftly dashed. Guido Menzel was the only batsman able to offer any resistance with a resolute 21. The damage was done by the medium pace of Charles Anton and William Deeley with four and three wickets respectively. The Germans were dismissed for an abject 56, though it might have been worse but for a stubborn 10 from Rolf Zickert at the bottom of the order. The spirit of the home team appeared to have finally been crushed.

Arthur Schmidt kept smiling, even though he must have been desperate to help his struggling teammates. He umpired in every match and the Gents grew to enjoy his geniality. At one stage during play he asked Dickie Williams what the colours signified on each of the different caps worn by the Englishmen. Some wore Gents colours, the Marlburians had their own, Whetherly wore his Harrovian cap and Huntington-Whiteley his Etonian one. Williams did his best to explain.

Schmidt was wearing a black and white cap to protect his ruddy face from the sun. Williams pointed at it.

'And who is your club?' he asked.

'Gunn and Moore,' replied Schmidt with a grin.

There is some confusion about the size of the crowd for this final match. *Reichssportblatt* thought the attendance was disappointing and admonished its readers for not showing up in larger numbers: 'But where were you, you masses who flock by the thousands to watch a game of football? This game also features "goals" (wickets), enough of them to give cricket a try. Think about this when the next football free period comes around!' In contrast, the *Berliner Morgenpost* commented on how well attended the matches had been, and favourably on the atmosphere. '[The matches] proved that this beautiful summer game could easily find more fans in Berlin and the rest of Germany, if only there would be yearly matches with English teams. At a Cricket match, sport is closely intertwined with relaxing outdoors – the matches are small parties with a familiar atmosphere.'

Whatever its size, the crowd were treated to stodgy fare on that last day. The Berliners looked to dig in and weren't bowled out until shortly before lunch. After the break the Gents went in search of quick runs to entertain the spectators and leave enough time to bowl the hosts out before the close of play. For once the gamble did not pay off. The Major sent in Robinson, Huntington-Whiteley and their guest Kuno Lehmann high up the order but all three were dismissed for ducks by the Menzel brothers. Felix also got rid of Whetherly and Young Maurice to end up with four of the eight wickets that fell before the Major declared with the score on 59. In the absence of full bowling figures we can't calculate Felix's bowling average or strike rate, but he had taken nine in this match and seventeen in the two he had played. He was by far the most successful bowler on the German side.

The question the Berliners faced was, could they bat out time and salvage a draw? To which the answer was, no. The innings started in familiar fashion: Huntington-Whiteley grabbed his customary two wickets in his opening spell and there was another run-out, this time Maus. The Major, fully recovered from his efforts of the day before, brought himself on and carnage ensued. He took five wickets, three of them caught by Peter Terry, who was even allowed a rare chance to bowl and took the wicket of Zehmke. Six of the Berlin side failed to add to the scorer's workload, and the team were bowled out for a humiliating 19 and a defeat of 249 runs. (Another account records the winning margin as a less grievous but still crushing 226 runs.)

With that, the two teams shook hands and the stumps were pulled on the Gents of Worcestershire tour to Berlin.

That evening the two teams came together for the last time at the dinner to honour the series at the Stadion-Terrassen restaurant* in the Olympic complex. The Reichssportführer

---

* The restaurant's address these days is Jesse-Owens-Allee. Suffice to say, back then it wasn't.

Hans von Tschammer und Osten was present, together with other Berlin sporting luminaries such as Dr Georg Xandry of the Deutsche Fussball Bund (and a Nazi party member). The Reichssportführer gave a speech in which, reportedly, he spoke a few words in halting English. 'Cricket is a very good game,' he said, doubtless reminiscing about his boozy afternoon at Lord's. 'I hope I may visit England to watch cricket in 1938.' He then presented the Major with a tie-pin emblazoned with a swastika. The Major kept hold of this until 1954 when he presented it to the Lord's museum (which has a record of its donation but no idea what happened to it subsequently).

The Major then gave a speech in which he thanked everyone for their hospitality and praised the spirit of his opponents. In order to improve, he suggested that the Berliners hire an English professional to coach local players the following summer, paying particular attention to their batting. After the speeches the men ate and the Major was able to speak privately with Tschammer und Osten, who seemed interested to know more about this idea of a coach. He then asked the Major if he had any other ideas about increasing interest in the game not just in Berlin but throughout Germany. Trying to be as diplomatic as possible, the Major suggested it might be beneficial if some of Berlin's senior players weren't so critical of fielding mistakes committed by younger members of the team. The Reichssportführer appeared unconvinced by this, so the Major reported the story he'd been told of Thamer punching one of the young players for dropping a catch, and hinted that that kind of behaviour might deter young men from taking up the game. 'Yes, I have heard about the incident,'

Tschammer und Osten said. 'But I understand it was a very simple catch.'

After dinner the two teams mingled, drank and swapped stories. Peter Robinson went around all present to collect signatures on the back of a booklet though, curiously, it wasn't signed by Felix Menzel. (Arthur Schmidt didn't sign it either, though Schneider, his fellow umpire, did, adding further evidence to the theory that he was Jewish.) At the end of the night, in the glow of friendship, they all shook hands and exchanged best wishes; some swapped addresses and invitations of hospitality should their new German friends ever find themselves in the Malverns. The Berliners were especially thankful. The Gents' visit, while it had been a sobering experience on the pitch, had attracted more press and attention than they had dreamed of. Only by playing more matches at this level could they improve.

Felix Menzel was determined the tour would be a beginning and not an end.

The Nord-Express to Ostend did not leave Friedrichstrasse until 9.22 on the evening of 12 August, which allowed the team a last day of sightseeing. Most went to the Zoological Gardens in the Tiergarten, but the senior members paid a visit to Cyril Smith. He was recovering well in hospital but it would be several more days before he was strong enough to return home. It's unknown if anyone stayed behind to keep him company or when and how he finally made it back to the UK. We do know from letters that it took some time for him to recover anything like full fitness. When war came he ran the local constabulary, almost certainly because he was not fit enough for frontline action.

As the team returned to the Adlon from their trips and excursions to collect their luggage, they noticed frenetic activity on the streets around the hotel. There was a different mood to the eeriness of the atmosphere on the night of the torchlight procession. Rather than parading in columns, troops were everywhere, stopping and searching passers-by, and there was the intermittent crackle of gunfire in the distance. Unknown to the Gents, Berlin was about to celebrate its seven hundredth anniversary (the date had been pulled out of thin air, the Nazis simply looking for an event to show their might);* an influx of visitors was expected and the authorities were rounding up and expelling 'undesirables'. The entire city had become even more fraught and uneasy, as if violence could erupt at any second. Even though it was a short taxi ride, it took an age for them to get to the station through the teeming streets. 'We were lucky and glad to get to the station,' Dickie Williams was to write.

The journey home took twenty-four hours – Peter Robinson arrived back in Upton shortly after nine p.m. on Friday, 13 August. 'Alas, the end of a wonderful ten days,' he wrote in his scrapbook.

If Geoffrey Tomkinson was fatigued by the tour or the journey home he didn't show it. The next day he played for Kidderminster Seconds against Trinity Road.

---

* Hitler showed his ambivalence towards the city by skipping the anniversary in favour of a festival celebrating his favourite composer, Richard Wagner, in Bayreuth, leaving Goebbels to milk the applause.

13

HEIL CRICKET!

THE *WORCESTER EVENING NEWS* printed the scorecards of the three matches and a brief interview with Robert Berkeley (mistakenly referring to him as 'Major') in which he spoke effusively about Berlin and the welcome they had received. 'Major Berkeley added that socially the touring side spent a most enjoyable time and all hoped they had given a little fillip to cricket in Germany.' He was less complimentary about the quality of the city's cricketers, describing the bowling and fielding as barely club standard while the batting was often worse.

Berkeley developed his theme in a summary of the tour written for *The Cricketer* winter annual. The batting was 'decidedly weak owing to a lack of coaching' and he supported the idea of a pro spending a summer there. 'Cricket cannot be learnt from a book; tuition and practice are essential.' He described the bowling of the two Menzel brothers as 'almost Veritian in steadiness; and it is remarkable how these two cricketers can bowl for three or four hours on end without losing their length'. The Berliners' other success was their fielding. 'The fielding is decidedly good, and in this respect special mention should be made of Herr Lehmann, who is particularly brilliant in any position.' Berkeley went on to underline the warmness of the Germans' hospitality and added that the tour 'will remain one of most pleasant memories'. 'Should the Germans ever send a side to England they can be quite certain they will be most welcome guests, especially to the Gentlemen of Worcestershire,' he concluded.

Back in Berlin the feeling was mutual. 'Auf Wiedersehen, Good Fellows,' wrote *Die Fußball-Woche* tearfully, expressing the hope that the visitors had returned home with a more positive impression of Nazi Germany than the one posted in the British press. The article also claimed that Tschammer und Osten was considering accepting the Gents' advice on hiring an English coach, and cited the example of several Canadian players who had spent time coaching and playing ice hockey in Germany. The Reichssportführer also wanted German exchange students in Britain to be initiated into the 'Mysterien des Kricket'. Despite the disappointment of being soundly beaten, the correspondent hoped that its small but persevering community would prosper and flourish in the future and that next summer might see more Englishmen playing cricket on German soil.

On 12 March 1938 the Wehrmacht marched into Hitler's homeland, Austria. Thousands of Berliners lined the streets to cheer and salute their leader on his return to Berlin four days after the 'reunification' of the two nations. The leaders of Europe's other major nations did nothing in response to this provocation. Their timid reaction confirmed Hitler's belief in both their weakness and his strength, and his hungry eyes turned to the Sudetenland and Czechoslovakia.

Felix Menzel had continued to dream through the winter of 1937/38, even as the fire lit by his leader threatened to become an inferno that might engulf Europe. His influence at the Reich's Ministry of Sport had not waned. There was no prospect of hiring an English pro, but he managed to persuade Tschammer und Osten to allow another English side to tour in the summer of 1938. Felix used the business connections of Francis Jordan, still living in Berlin, to find a club willing to come.

The eventual tourists, the Somerset Wanderers, were drawn from four club sides in the West Country: Crewkerne, Martock, South Petherton and Yeovil. They were not as illustrious, wealthy or as talented as the Gents team of the previous summer, but the Berliners were seeking a closer contest so that was no bad thing. Led by Dick Welch and assisted by their honorary secretary Len Pitcher, the team travelled to Berlin on Saturday, 30 July via Dover, Ostend and Cologne and arrived in Berlin the following evening, where they were met by Felix Menzel.

The publicity of the previous summer had been instructive and Felix had learned well. The day after the Wanderers' arrival he invited the German sporting press to a lunch to welcome the visitors, though his target was a much wider audience. In a speech he made a direct pitch to the MCC, asking them to stage an international tournament to help promote cricket on the continent. 'The cup would be played for in England by an MCC side, and teams from the continent such as Germany, Belgium, Holland and Denmark. Of course, the British team would win, but the following year she would have to defend the cup in one of the other countries. This would give wonderful impetus to cricket on the Continent, and would provide an opportunity of British and Continental cricketers getting to know each other.' There was an irony in Felix promoting a tournament that might help unite Europe at the same time as the leader of his country was busy sowing the seeds of a conflict that would tear it apart. 'With football and similar games the atmosphere in which the games are contested is so strenuous and passionate, but cricket is so soothing and peaceful,' he added. In effect he was proposing an international cricket tournament thirty-nine years before such an event was first held.

The response was better than Felix could have dreamed of. Reuters picked up the story and put it on their wire; it ran in several national newspapers in England, including *The Times*. 'An Appeal to the M.C.C.' ran its headline, rather more subtly and accurately than the *Daily Mirror*'s 'Heil Cricket, say Nazis'. 'Germany has gone all cricket conscious, wants to boost the summer game,' the *Mirror*'s article read. 'They've got a cricket fuehrer, Herr Felix Mensel [*sic*], and he's asked the MCC to put up a trophy for international competition.' The story even reached the Australian press: both the Melbourne *Age* and the *Canberra Times* reported Felix's request. In one short speech he had managed to achieve more favourable press coverage for his country than anything Goebbels had produced. No reply was forthcoming from the MCC, however.

There are few existing records of the Somerset Wanderers tour. No scorecards survive. Three matches were played: the first against Felix Menzel's team, Preussen CC, and the second against BSV 92, captained by his brother Guido; a final match took place on the Schenkendorfplatz at the Olympic Stadium. In the first game the Wanderers scored 204 for 6 in their first innings before bowling the home side out for 46, twenty-seven of which came from Felix's bat. Preussen put up sterner resistance when they were asked to follow on and were 70 for 5 when a thunderstorm washed out the rest of the day's play. After their drubbing by the Gents, a rain-affected draw was a creditable result.

Two days later, on 5 August, at the BSV 92 stadium in Schmargendorf, the Wanderers again batted first and knocked up a similar score, 203 for 6, before declaring. Like their predecessors from Worcestershire, they were shocked to see senior German players like Thamer scolding the younger ones for poor fielding and treating dropped catches as blots on their national honour, which suggests little heed had been paid to the Major's pep talk the previous summer. BSV slumped to 61 and 70 all out and lost by 72 runs.

Like their Worcestershire counterparts, the Somerset team were treated very well off the pitch. Little is known of their itinerary on their off days other than a visit to the largest milk factory in Europe, which must have been fun. Rather more attractive were the 'biergartens' of Berlin, where the side reportedly spent much of their time. This over-indulgence might explain their disappointing performance in the last match, though the combined Berlin XI provided a sterner test. For the first time in two summers the Berliners batted first; it didn't improve their fortunes and they were dismissed for 77. Thanks to the accurate bowling of both Menzel brothers, the Wanderers were unable to force themselves into a winning position. They declared on 87 for 7 and at the end of the match the home team had reached 90 for 6. With the game well poised it was a shame there was not a second day, but after being trounced the year before the Germans were understandably reluctant to risk any more two-day hidings.

The tour concluded with a dinner at the Hotel Russischer

Hof, hosted by Obergrüppenführer Hans Breithaupt rather than Tschammer und Osten. The SS man presented the Somerset side with a porcelain statue of a lion mounted on an ebony base, which doubled as a bookend at Len Pitcher's house for several decades. The West Country men responded with a rousing rendition of 'Up from Somerset' by Frederic Weatherly, who also wrote the lyrics to 'Danny Boy'. With hindsight, the final verse seems prophetic:

> For we'm come up from Somerset,
> Where the cider apples grow,
> For we're all King's men in Somerset,
> As they were long, long ago.
> An' when you're wanting soldier boys,
> An' there's fighting for to do,
> You just send word to Somerset,
> An' we'll all be up for you!

English teams were not the only touring sides Felix Menzel was able to lure to Berlin. The Old Boys of Copenhagen played a match against a Berlin XI on Sunday, 29 August 1937 at BSV 92's ground. The home team ran out convincing winners by 107 runs, scoring 133 and 98 to their opponents' 90 and 34. The Menzel brothers (another brother, Leo, also played in this match) were the heroes: they took nine of the ten wickets to fall in the Old Boys' second innings. The following year they travelled to Copenhagen for a return fixture and were victorious once more. On that late June day Guido Menzel scored 84 (believed to have been the highest score by a German national at that time) in a first-innings total of 223. The Old Boys replied with 126 and were then asked to chase 160 for victory. They were bowled out for 85. (Coincidentally, Copenhagen was the choice for the Gents' annual tour of 1938.)

At that stage, even with the sounds of war rumbling in the distance, Felix was still confident that cricket had the potential to become an established sport in his home country. His plan was to invite an English touring side each summer bookended by regular fixtures against Danish sides home and away, all the while persisting with his idea for an inter-European tournament. But his vision was fatally undermined by the Sudeten crisis of 1938 and the cataclysmic events that followed. Hitler marched unopposed into Czechoslovakia, against the will of most of its people but again without protest from Britain and France. After returning from making a pact with Hitler in Munich, Prime Minister Neville Chamberlain famously declared it was 'peace in our time' and vowed that British men and women could sleep quietly in their beds.

Pyrrhic though this declaration was, there was no re-assurance whatsoever for the inhabitants of Berlin, the dwindling, beleaguered Jewish community in particular. On the night of 9/10 November 1938 Hitler's SA heavies, assisted by civilians, carried out a series of brutal coordinated attacks on Jewish homes, businesses and places of worship. So much shattered glass littered the streets that the pogrom became known as Kristallnacht ('Crystal Night'). Scores were killed and hundreds of thousands deported to concentration camps.

As 1938 gave way to 1939 the persecution of the Jews intensified. Hundreds of thousands were deported and those who remained suffered one indignity after another. New tenancy laws abolished any protection and they were forced to give their houses and apartments to 'Aryans' whose houses had been demolished as part of Hitler's and Albert Speer's transformation of Berlin into Germania. That same year an Arthur Schmidt born around the same time as 'Mauschel Schmidt' moved to Sophienstrasse in central Berlin. It was a predominantly Jewish district, and it was likely that he was evicted from his own property and forced to move there.

Kristallnacht laid bare to the world the aggressively racist nature of Hitler's regime. When the Führer invaded the rest of Czechoslovakia in March 1939, Chamberlain's appeasement policy was revealed as futile. As the summer of 1939 approached war seemed inevitable. But *still* Felix Menzel refused to give up. He managed to arrange a visit by Nykobing Falster of Denmark in late July. They were not a strong team, but it was a game of cricket and another chance for the Berliners to pit their skills against foreign opposition. Teams from Preussen and BSV and a combined eleven recorded convincing wins. Very little is known of the scores other than that Guido Menzel took eleven wickets in one match played on 29 and 30 July, including three in the last five minutes of play.

On 1 September, Hitler invaded Poland. Typically, he didn't even have the decency to wait until the end of the cricket season. Two days later Britain and France declared war on Germany. This marked an end to organized cricket in the country and the death of Felix Menzel's dream. The blazing summer of 1937 when Englishmen came and played friendly games of cricket now seemed a lifetime ago. For many who played in those unofficial 'Tests', life would never be the same again.

14

SHADOWS OF WAR

In *A Social History of English Cricket*, Derek Birley states when writing about the outbreak of the Second World War, 'There had been much talk in the 1930s, not all of it in jest, about the unfortunate circumstances that the Germans did not play cricket.' Had they experienced the civilizing influence of the game, the argument went, the Germans might not have been so keen to seek conflict and any problems between the countries might have been resolved elsewhere rather than on the battlefield. As we know, the Germans *did* play cricket, and certainly men like Felix Menzel believed wholeheartedly in the game's soothing qualities and the opportunities it presented to unite men of different nations.

At the outset of war there was a sense in Britain that another, more serious game had begun. Sir Home Gordon, the colourful correspondent who had written the article in *The Cricketer* that announced the Gents' tour to Berlin, turned to cricketing metaphor to address the grave situation: 'England has now begun the grim Test match . . . we do not wish merely to win the ashes of civilisation. We want to win a lasting peace with honour and prosperity to us all.' He was not alone in indulging in this sort of imagery: a cartoon appeared in the *Evening Standard* depicting Neville Chamberlain as a trembling batsman about to face the bowling of Hitler and Mussolini, armed with grenades rather than cricket balls.

The MCC and the counties agreed unanimously that county cricket should be suspended for the duration of the war. Both The Oval and Lord's were turned over to the Army and RAF as inspection centres for processing and examining new recruits. More than one enlistee recounted the story of being told to drop his trousers in the Long Room to be inspected for sexually transmitted diseases as the great ghosts of the game looked on.

While the hallowed grounds of English cricket were deployed in the war effort, away from the first-class arena the game continued as normally as it could: counties played friendlies against each other; the Northern leagues were stacked with first-class talent; the public schools fulfilled their annual fixtures; the game's bible, *Wisden*, was still published each year, though in a limited edition due to 'war rationing'; and, of course, the sound of leather on willow continued to be heard on village greens up and down the country. During the 'phoney war' of 1939/40 when those at home were almost able to forget there was a war on there was even talk of reviving the county championship. But those ambitions were thwarted by the Blitz and Hitler's triumphant march through Belgium and France. By 1941 England stood alone – 'Last man at the crease, in fading light, the opposition with their tails up, on a darned sticky wicket', as Sir Home Gordon might have put it. Yet even in those dark days, as if obeying some atavistic urge Englishmen insisted on playing cricket. One refugee from Vichy France travelling on a train to London gazed from his window into the dappled sunlight and saw 'all along the line young men in flannels . . . playing cricket in the sunshine on beautifully tended fields shaded by oaks and poplar trees'.

Professional cricket suffered its casualties, most famously Hedley Verity, the great Yorkshire and England left-arm spinner, who was wounded during the Allied invasion of Sicily in 1943 and died in a POW camp; and Essex's Ken Farnes, a former Test bowling partner of Verity, who joined the RAF and was killed when his aircraft crashed during a night-flying exercise. Many others served and survived, while thousands of amateur cricketers perished.

Some matches were played at Lord's amid the falling bombs, which killed an estimated thirty thousand people in the capital. The Army played regular fixtures against the RAF. During one match in 1944 play was halted when the players and spectators heard the sound of a V-1 in the distance. As the sound grew louder, the players flung themselves to the ground. The bomb exploded nearby, play resumed, and Middlesex batsman Jack Robertson hit the first ball after the stoppage for six, as if in defiance of the Nazis. The *Wisden* almanack of 1945 showed two photographs of the event, captioned 'Flying Bomb Stops Play'.

Cricket continued in far-flung corners of the empire, too. Denis Compton was stationed in India and ended up playing in the Ranji Trophy Final, scoring 249 not out for Holkar against Bombay. Matches took place on even more unfamiliar soil. In his autobiography Yorkshire fast bowler Bill Bowes recounted how he and several other professional cricketers – among them Freddie Brown, later an England captain – were captured and held in a prisoner-of-war camp in Italy, where they managed to stage an unofficial Ashes match between English and Australian prisoners and even built a makeshift scoreboard. Due to malnutrition and fatigue they were only able to play for an hour or two each day, but even under such hellish conditions it was taken as seriously as any Ashes encounter. At another POW camp, in Spangenberg, the journalist and author Terence Prittie sent to *The Cricketer* several articles on and scorecards from matches he and other prisoners played. At first they were stopped by the censor, who feared that 'O.M.W.R. and A.' was some kind of code. Eventually William Joyce, the traitorous British toff turned Nazi supporter known more famously as Lord Haw-Haw, pointed out that the letters stood for 'Overs, Maidens, Wickets, Runs and Average', after which Prittie's reports were allowed through.

So not even incarceration could prevent Englishmen (well, an Irishman in Prittie's case) playing cricket.

Berliners had been fed a stream of lies by Goebbels' propaganda machine in the run-up to war. Most had been eager to swallow them. The Germans viewed themselves as defenders, not aggressors, guilty only of claiming back territory that was rightfully theirs. Despite this conviction there was none of the jubilation and defiance in 1939 that had greeted the outbreak of war in 1914. Berliners were resigned and weary; there was 'no excitement, no hurrahs, no cheering, no throwing of flowers, no war fever, no war hysteria', wrote the American foreign correspondent William Shirer. But the rapid conquests of Poland, Denmark, Norway, the Low Countries and, above all, France raised their spirits and they began to dream of a quick end to a war that had barely touched them. There was some rationing but daily life had remained much the same and the flow of good news from the front kept the public mood buoyant.

Football continued to give the masses an outlet, but there

was no appetite for cricket in the summer of 1940. None apart from in the belly of one man, that is. In those first few years of what Germans called *Sitzkrieg* (the 'sitting war'), and even after the disastrous decision to invade the Soviet Union, which meant the Wehrmacht was fighting fronts in the west, east and in North Africa as well as places like Yugoslavia, Felix Menzel still dreamed of getting a game on. His main problem was a lack of bodies. He and his brother Guido, Alfred Ladwig and 1930 tour all-rounder Franz Hustan were all too old to fight, but the younger generation had been sent to the front: Kurt Rietz, Gustav Parnemann, Egon Maus, Kuno Lehmann, Gerhard Thamer, the Dartsch brothers, Rolf Zickert and Willi Mesecke all saw combat.

As the advance in the Soviet Union stalled in the mud and snow and more men were needed to serve, Germany started to import forced foreign labour to fill the shortage in the market. Many of these workers were from occupied Eastern Europe, but others were brought in from Holland and Belgium. These men worked on major building projects and in armament factories and were treated no better than slaves. Of the three hundred thousand sent to Berlin almost half perished through hunger, disease or in bombing raids. The purity of German blood was to be protected at all costs and there were draconian punishments for anyone caught fraternizing with these foreign workers without good reason. Between 1940 and 1942 the German *Volk* were bombarded with pamphlets instructing them to keep their distance and women were threatened with imprisonment or worse if they dared to have sex with these outsiders.

Dire threats weren't enough to deter Felix Menzel from making their acquaintance. The *Ostarbeiter* (workers) from Eastern Europe had no cricketing culture, but a few military internees from Denmark and Holland did. Felix managed to find them and a few Indians ('who were staying in Berlin for reasons unknown to me', he later wrote)* and, remarkably, played a few games of cricket. '[I] got together Dutch and Danish workmen and . . . with the few remaining Germans we brought about very good cricket matches, highly interesting to all concerned.' Had they been discovered, it's likely the Gestapo would also have found them 'highly interesting'. But either he managed to escape their all-seeing eye or he found a way to persuade them it was harmless fun.

As was the case with Bill Bowes and his fellow POWs, it seemed as if nothing, not even the barbarity of war, was going to stop Felix Menzel indulging his love of cricket.

There is no record of the Gentlemen of Worcestershire playing any wartime matches, though it would be surprising if they didn't play the occasional match to show the Jerries that British life would continue as normal. Almost all of the squad that toured Berlin were involved in the war effort. Some senior players were too old for combat, but something as arbitrary as age wasn't going to prevent the Major from serving his country. True to his Captain Mainwaring role he took charge of the local battalion of the Home Guard.

* There's a good chance that the Indians Menzel referred to were part of the Indische Legion (Indian Legion), an Indian unit trained and raised in Germany in 1941. Many were Indian students who were resident in Germany and chose to stay, and then volunteered. Others were Indian POWs captured by Rommel during his North Africa campaign.

Neither, as a decorated veteran of the Great War, was Geoffrey Tomkinson going to sit idly by. So many policemen were required to fight that special constabularies had been formed across the country as cover, and Tomkinson took command of his local one. From September 1939 until he was forced to stand down in 1941 at the age of sixty he was enrolled in the Army Officers Emergency Reserve. But while age curtailed his availability for service, it didn't end his cricket career. He continued to serve Kidderminster as a hard-hitting batsman in the Birmingham League throughout the war years and his stroke-making ability occasionally flared into life. In one match he came up against ex-England seamer Reg Perks, the mainstay of Worcestershire's bowling attack for two decades. Tomkinson smashed an unbeaten 74; at one stage during the innings Perks had six men stationed in the outfield to stop the barrage of boundaries.

Some of the senior players did see action. Even though he was approaching forty-seven when the war started, William Deeley re-entered the Royal Army Signal Corps, where he rose to the rank of Major and served with such distinction that the Lieutenant General of 9th Corps recommended him for an operational MBE. In his citation for the award in 1943 he wrote:

An Officer of outstanding character and ability who possesses unequalled powers of leadership. His zeal and devotion to duty have been exceptional and an example to those serving with him. This Officer has served under me for nearly three years in this war as a Staff Officer and unit commander. With the B.E.F. [British Expeditionary Force] in France his unit performed outstanding work and by his example and coolness under the difficult conditions prevailing on the beaches was successful in bringing his unit back to England intact. As a unit commander his outstanding qualities have always been a guidance and example to officers and men alike.

The 'difficult conditions* prevailing on the beaches' was a reference to Operation Dynamo, the 'Miracle of Dunkirk' – the attempt in May and June 1940 to rescue vast numbers of British and Allied troops who had been trapped and cut off by the German forces. Deeley and his unit were among hundreds of thousands of men who had to wade shoulder deep into the water to reach ships to take them to safety while under attack by German forces on land and in the air.

Among the flotilla of 'little ships' that rescued the soldiers from the beaches was a ship familiar to Deeley, the *Prince Baudouin*, which in less bloody times had carried the Gents from Dover to Ostend and back again. It was moored in Ostend when the Germans invaded Belgium and sailed for the UK with a mass of refugees on board while under attack from the Luftwaffe. The ship managed to reach Southampton intact and was transferred to the Ministry of War. After evacuating troops from the beaches of Brest, Cherbourg and St Malo during the Dunkirk retreat it was used to transport troops to the Mediterranean and North Africa.

The ship's story does not end there. Four years after

* This phrase is a classic piece of English understatement. German planes bombed and strafed the exposed troops on the beaches and an estimated twenty to thirty thousand were wounded or killed. Approximately forty thousand more were left behind and taken prisoner.

Dunkirk it transported troops to France for Operation
Overlord, the Allied invasion of mainland Europe. This time
its cargo was US troops from the 5th Rangers Battalion.
The *Prince Baudouin* arrived shortly after dawn to drop the
soldiers at Omaha Beach where they were met by intense
German gunfire – a scene immortalized in the Steven
Spielberg movie *Saving Private Ryan*. Its final assignment
came a month later, in July 1944, when it landed troops in the
south of France. At the end of the war it was returned to the
Belgian government.

Peter Robinson was on board another ship in the
Channel on D-Day. He had left Marlborough in 1938 and
gone straight into the Royal Navy as a regular. In 1941 he
worked on the Arctic convoys, one of the most unheralded
yet crucial efforts of the war: this fleet of ships delivered
vital supplies to blockaded parts of the Soviet Union to equip
them in their fight with Germany. The convoys braved ice
and extreme cold, all the while risking attack from German
U-boats and aircraft. One convoy, PQ 17, lost eleven of its
thirty-five vessels when it scattered following rumours that
a huge German fleet was on its tail, including the legendary
battleship the *Tirpitz*.

Robinson survived, though. After the freezing seas of
the Arctic his next posting was on the warmer waters of the
Mediterranean, where he took part in Combined Operations
as part of the North African Flotilla seeking to drive the
German and Italian armies out of the region. Then he was
sent back to Europe to take part in the Normandy landings.
While the war on the beaches raged he was stationed on a
battleship anchored at sea. According to his son Henry, he
always felt a tinge of shame that while that coastline was

awash with the blood of their brothers-in-arms he and his fellow officers were changing for dinner on board their ship, eating and drinking as if nothing was happening.

Like his friend and neighbour Peter Robinson, Young Maurice Jewell also left Marlborough in 1938 and went straight into the armed forces. He chose the Army and was made a 2nd Lieutenant in the Worcestershire Royal Territorial Army. Once war broke out he joined the 10th Worcestershire Regiment and served in Northern Ireland, where he was promoted to Temporary Captain and appointed as an instructor in a battle school. Perhaps keen to see some action, he transferred to the Royal Tank Regiment in 1944.

A month after returning from Berlin, Peter Terry went to Pembroke College, Cambridge; though he was not awarded a cricket Blue he did play for the Crusaders, effectively the university's second XI. He also started for the Gentlemen of Yorkshire and scored a career-high 149 against Eton Ramblers only a few weeks before war broke out. At the start of his third year he signed up for the Suffolk Regiment in Bury St Edmunds and performed his training there before transferring to the West Yorkshire Regiment in York, near his family home, in late 1940. He spent most of the war as a training instructor at Catterick in North Yorkshire, where he became heavily involved in Army sports. Only in 1945, when he was posted to the 1st Indian Airborne Division near Nagpur, did it look as if he might see frontline action. His regiment was among those preparing for a final assault on Japanese forces in the Far East. However, the bombing of Hiroshima and Nagasaki brought about the Japanese surrender before that was necessary and he left the Army as a Captain in 1946.

The 1937 tour's very own Captain, Robert Berkeley, was another of the older brigade who saw military action, with the Royal Artillery, though the details of his service have been lost. C. S. Anton served with the Royal Regiment of Artillery and later became Honorary Colonel and finally Colonel Anton, but the theatres in which he fought are also unknown. The only member of the eleven whose war record I couldn't find (I shall come to the exploits of Robin Whetherly and Peter Huntington-Whiteley in a moment) is Dickie Williams, who was born too late to fight in the First World War and too early to take part in the Second. It's likely he served in the Home Guard but there is no record of it.

The onset of war brought more terror for Berlin's remaining Jews in the form of anti-Semitic ordinance upon ordinance, humiliation upon humiliation, and horror upon horror. In 1939 they were subjected to an eight p.m. curfew and their radio sets were confiscated. The next year their ration cards for shoes and clothing were stopped; they were permitted to shop for only one hour each day, between four and five p.m.; then their telephones were taken away; and they were forced to hide from Allied bombs in less secure shelters, separated from other Berliners. In 1941 came perhaps the worst indignity of the lot: all Jews were forced to wear a yellow star to identify themselves. They were banned from using public transport and forbidden to leave the country.

In January 1942, at a villa directly across the water from the same Wannsee beach where the Gents had swum and sunbathed fewer than five years earlier, a group of senior Nazi officials met to discuss the fate of European Jews. The Wannsee Conference, as it has become known, agreed the implementation of the Final Solution – the plan to exterminate every Jew in German-occupied Europe at concentration camps in Poland. The first train to leave Berlin for Auschwitz carrying some of the city's sixty to seventy thousand Jews departed on 11 July. The locals did nothing to stop this tragedy. 'Many Berliners turned away as the columns of Jews walked quietly to the stations or were loaded on to trucks late in the evening.'*

Many Jews who saw what was coming committed suicide. Others continued to harbour the delusion that the country which had been their family's home for centuries wouldn't kill them; they believed they were on their way to start a new life in the east. By 11 March 1943 more than half of the Berlin Jewish community had been taken east, to Auschwitz, and most had been gassed in its death chambers. Goebbels was determined to declare Berlin *Judenfrei*. By 19 May he claimed to have achieved his aim.

A month earlier, on 19 April, on transport 37, an Arthur Schmidt was deported to Auschwitz from Gleis 17 of Berlin Grunewald station. He too was gassed to death. Was this 'Mauschel' Schmidt, the slow left-arm scourge of Dartford CC, the 'Sobek of cricket'? We cannot be sure, though his age fits. There was only one other Jewish Arthur Schmidt in Berlin at that time of the right age. Mercifully, he survived the Holocaust, though few details are known about him. Perhaps

* This quotation, and another later in this chapter about the Soviet 'liberators', come from Alexandra Richie's *Faust's Metropolis*.

he was one of the 'lucky' few who were spared because they had married privileged Aryan men or women. We can only pray that man was 'Mauschel'. But there is good evidence that the Germans, after years of subjecting him to humiliation and abuse, sent the finest cricketer they ever possessed to the death camps.

On the day Britain declared war on Germany, Robin Whetherly was travelling on the *Aquitania* from New York to Southampton. Since leaving university he had been working for Swan's Travel Bureau of Russell Square. W. F. Swan, its founder, was an early travel entrepreneur who organized land tours in Europe to places like France and Flanders to visit graves of British soldiers killed in the First World War. By the time of the Second World War much of his business comprised arranging sea passage for European refugees fleeing Hitler's advancing armies. Whetherly was lucky to be on the *Aquitania*. Had the dice rolled differently he might have been on board *Athenia,* en route to Canada with forty-two of Swan's passengers when it was torpedoed by a U-boat, thus becoming the first British ship to be sunk by the Germans in the Second World War.

Upon his return Whetherly accepted a commission into the King's Dragoon Guards, the celebrated cavalry regiment which had only swapped horses for tanks in 1937. He was immediately posted to the Middle East where his regiment was given the job of patrolling the Libyan border. He was part of the offensive that forced the attacking Italian Army back four hundred miles, in the process capturing a hundred thousand men and a mass of enemy equipment. As a result Whetherly was promoted to Lieutenant.

The Germans, led by General Erwin Rommel, responded by landing units at Benghazi in early April 1941; Whetherly and his troops were the first Allied forces to engage his Afrika-Corps. It was a salutary experience. The KDG came under continuous attack from land and air and were forced to retreat in chaos on difficult terrain. On 5 April the brigade's convoy of lorries and its petrol dump were destroyed by bombs dropped by German aircraft; facing a fuel shortage, they withdrew further to the east under the cover of darkness, heading for the town of Derna. The town was a mass of people and vehicles, which hindered their progress. Their objective was to take the aerodrome nearby, though by now the enemy was closing in.

Whetherly's orders were to take two armoured cars of troops to offer support to an infantry division guarding the perimeter of the aerodrome. By the time he arrived the Germans had started to shell the aerodrome and roads leading from it. The bombardment increased and Whetherly moved his position from the east of the airfield to its north, where he was able to hit back with artillery and small-arms fire on German positions. This eased the pressure on troops inside the aerodrome and on nearby roads who had become sitting ducks for the German guns. After being given the order to evacuate his troops, Whetherly risked his life trying to save the crews who had escaped from a group of stricken lorries that had been struck by enemy shells.

Whetherly then turned his focus on the surviving lorries. He was taking them eastwards when a Messerschmitt strafed the small convoy, destroying more vehicles, wounding five of his men and killing another. He and two men treated the injured and hoisted them into the remaining trucks. On the road out he rode in the remaining armoured car and acted as a flank guard to his convoy. He managed to get three lorries to safety and saved more than a hundred men from capture. While Whetherly was saving his men, much of the rest of the regiment was captured and forced to surrender to Rommel.

For his actions, Whetherly was awarded the Military Cross. General (later Field Marshal) Archibald Wavell, who led the Western Desert Force, wrote this citation: 'There is no doubt that the coolness displayed by this officer enabled the infantry on the aerodrome to withdraw by drawing most of the fire from the enemy's guns . . . and resulted in saving the lives and preventing the capture of a considerable number of men.' Wavell went on to praise Whetherly's 'great courage'. 'This officer, during the eight weeks that his squadron has been in Libya, has shown considerable skill and coolness on several occasions . . . and during patrol work has produced much useful information often under severe attacks from the air. His courage and coolness have been a very fine example to all ranks.'

Now with an MC after his name, Whetherly and the remains of his regiment were stationed near Cairo for the summer of 1941, which gave him a chance to play a few games of cricket at the Gezira Club, a tranquil and exclusive retreat for officers only. Its green fields, firs from Aberdeen, azaleas from Sussex and beds of London lavender must have been a balm for Whetherly's heat- and dust-blasted eyes. No records of those matches have survived, but we do know that several fiercely contested games took place, often along national lines: English officers playing South Africans, Kiwis and Aussies. Whetherly returned to the Western Desert only a few weeks before future Australia captain Lindsay Hassett arrived with his regiment. (The pair had met on the field in 1938 when Whetherly played for Oxford University against the touring Australians. Hassett scored 146.)

By now Whetherly was a Temporary Major and took command of a squadron. He participated in Operation Crusader, which succeeded in relieving the siege of Tobruk and gave the British ground forces their first victory of the war. He also led a regiment that played a part in halting Rommel's offensive in 1942. From that point on Whetherly's men ranged across Egypt, though they missed the Battle of El-Alamein.

By mid 1943 the war in North Africa was over; but Whetherly's talents would not go unnoticed or unused. He was selected to serve with the Special Operations Executive. His 'application form' for the SOE reveals that when he was on leave back in England his permanent address was the Cavalry Club on Piccadilly, where he had been a member since 1940 – which gives an indication of his private wealth.

In September 1943, Whetherly parachuted into Yugoslavia to join Brigadier Fitzroy Maclean's mission to liaise with Tito and his band of Partisans, who were thwarting Hitler's plans to take control of the Balkans. Their job, on orders from Winston Churchill, was 'simply to find out who was killing the most Germans and suggest means by which we could help them to kill more', according to Maclean. Despite being a baronet and a Conservative MP, not to mention one of the growing band of men said to have inspired Ian Fleming's creation of James Bond, Maclean grew to respect Tito and his communist fighters because of their tenacious and brave resistance in the face of fascism. Whetherly also made an instant impression on him: '[Whetherly] had a first-class record as a fighting soldier with the K.D.G.s in the desert and whom, as our only cavalry officer, we promised to put in charge of the first horses, or alternatively armoured vehicles, that we captured.'

September became October and the Yugoslavian winter started to bite. Maclean left Tito and Whetherly behind to report back on his mission. The order came through to try and fly a Partisan delegation to Cairo for a conference to discuss future plans, so Maclean prepared to head back. 'Very cold here,' Whetherly signalled to Maclean. 'Please bring rum ration.' The cold weather and thick cloud prevented Maclean from landing despite several attempts. In his absence, Whetherly, another young officer Captain Donald Knight and Captain Bill Deakins decided to build a makeshift airstrip near Glamoc and fly out the young Partisan leader Lola Ribar, Tito's personal delegate, and his party. November arrived and the airstrip was ready; when the Partisans managed to steal a small German bomber and hide it, the operation was on.

At dawn on the 27th the party gathered on a 'bleak, wind-swept plain'. The bomber had been brought to Glamoc the night before, fuelled, and the RAF and anti-aircraft batteries notified not to fire on a small Dornier fighter with German markings. The engine took some time to start in the freezing air but soon they were ready to leave. A small farewell party had gathered to see the delegation off.

Suddenly there was the sound of an engine drone in the sky above. The party looked to the crest of a nearby hill and spotted a small German observation plane. They turned to run for cover but it was above them before they could move, two small bombs tumbling from its belly. One landed directly on the aircraft, killing Knight and Ribar instantly; the second hit the ground near Whetherly and Deakins without exploding and rolled towards them 'like a football'. Whetherly saw it first and grabbed his colleague's arm to warn him. Deakins threw himself to the ground as the bomb exploded.

Robin was killed instantly: he had not been quick enough. The split second he had taken to warn Deakins had saved his friend's life but cost him his own. 'It was sad news indeed,' wrote Maclean. 'In Robin Whetherly and Donald Knight I had lost two good friends and two of my best officers.' Subsequent intelligence revealed the operation to fly Ribar out had been betrayed by a traitor. That afternoon the bodies of Whetherly and the two other men were buried side by side on a hill overlooking Glamoc. Their remains were later transferred to the Belgrade war cemetery.

In December 1943, Major Linn 'Slim' Farrish of the US Army wrote to Robin's parents. 'I was an American representative with the same Mission, and Robin and I became close friends under field conditions,' he told them. 'To me he was indicative of all that is worthwhile in this sometimes amazing intricate struggle . . . Perhaps fine boys like Robin have to be taken from us in order to bring us to our senses, and to engender within us the high resolve to make something out of all this misunderstanding. I shall do what I can in my small way towards this end, and Robin's memory will give me courage and incentive to carry on.' Farrish, of whom it has recently been alleged that he was passing information on Allied movements to Soviet intelligence, was killed in 1944 when his aircraft crashed in the Balkans.

In June 1944, Peter Huntington-Whiteley returned to the Agar's Plough playing field to represent the Eton Ramblers against the College. It must have brought back fond memories of opening the bowling for the school on the old ground in more carefree days. He even had family in the crowd: his youngest brother Miles was at Eton and had made the short walk along the high street to watch. The main attraction was former England captain and conscientious objector to Douglas Jardine's Bodyline tactics Gubby Allen, who scored 103 for the Ramblers. The match had been scheduled for two days but was completed in one with the College running out winners by 44 runs. Peter didn't get to bat or bowl but that surely didn't matter; it was a respite from war, in which he'd played a major role.

After the match he headed back to his unit, and three days later he took part in the invasion of Normandy.

Huntington-Whiteley had played a final season for the College in 1938. 'H. O. Huntington-Whiteley, of whom great things were expected, proved disappointing,' was *Wisden*'s deflating verdict on his campaign. He went straight into the Royal Marines as a 2nd Lieutenant and completed his paratrooper training. On the face of it, despite his height and athletic abilities, he did not seem the world's most natural soldier; he was diffident, almost too laid back, with a dry, playful sense of humour. But this coolness would serve him well in combat.

The details of his first two years of war service are unknown, but he must have impressed. In 1942, when Ian Fleming – later the creator of James Bond but at this time a senior figure in British naval intelligence – was tasked with forming a special commando unit to search out, forage for and steal enemy intelligence, he handpicked a group of the finest soldiers available to command it, and among them was the tall, languid Huntington-Whiteley, or 'Red' as he was known to his brothers-in-arms because of his distinctive hair colour.

No. 30 Commando's* first assignment was Operation Jubilee, a daring and ambitious plan by a combined Anglo-Canadian land and naval force to seize Dieppe, destroy military targets, grab intelligence, take prisoners and then retreat. The Allied leaders' aim was to dent German defences on mainland Europe. For too long Britain had been on the back foot, living in fear of German invasion. A successful raid would prove it was capable of opening a second front in France and provide a much-needed morale boost at home.

Fleming did not fight but directed operations from the rear. His unit, led by Huntington-Whiteley, planned to ghost into a quayside hotel which acted as a local HQ for the German Navy and snatch as much enemy intelligence as possible. The main prize was an Enigma machine, which Fleming then planned to transport back to the code-breakers at Bletchley Park, at top speed.

According to Nicholas Rankin, the author of *Ian Fleming's Commandos: The Story of 30 Assault Unit in WWII*, 'Dieppe seemed a beautiful plan: great in theory, good-looking on

* The unit was later known as 30 Assault Unit.

paper.' In reality it turned out to be a disaster. They found the enemy well prepared, the beaches they landed on were difficult to traverse, and supremacy in the air was beyond them; thousands of men were shot and killed in a hail of bullets and battery fired from the shores and cliffs above the beach. One Canadian regiment lost a staggering 90 per cent of its men, wounded or captured on the aptly named Red Beach – the same beach on which 10 Platoon, led by Huntington-Whiteley, were to land.

At 8.30 a.m. the flotilla made its way towards land. They were soon engulfed in shellfire and smoke. As the Dieppe shoreline emerged from the haze, their landing craft was hit by a shell and burst into flames, spilling the men into the sea. They were given a split-second choice: swim towards death and mayhem on the nearer shore, or turn and swim further to their ships and relative safety. Most chose the latter, though Huntington-Whiteley and others were picked up by a flak craft. Only after the effects of the freezing water had worn off did they notice the burns to their legs. The entire raid had been a disaster, though the bloody lessons learned were used in preparation for Operation Overlord two years later.

It was an inauspicious beginning for Fleming's unit. But the powers-that-be decided it was worth persevering with. Huntington-Whiteley was given the responsibility of inter-viewing and picking new men. Would-be recruits arrived at the unit's office in Whitehall trembling at the prospect of meeting a ferocious special ops Royal Marines officer only to be met by Huntington-Whiteley's kind smile and informal manner. He stood up to shake their hand and invited rather than ordered them to sit down. Once training began at their base in Littlehampton they became familiar with his wit, too.

One recruit recalled going into troop HQ and hearing Red answer the phone with the words, 'Hello, Littlehampton Toy Shop here.' There was a pause. 'Oh, yes sir, I see sir,' he said. 'Certainly, Colonel.'

The Dieppe Raid was a mere blip for 30 Assault Unit. Their job was now well defined: join an attacking force and capture as much intelligence as possible. In 1943 they operated with great success in Norway, Sicily, Italy and the Greek islands before returning to the UK to prepare for the Allied invasion of Europe. In early 1944 Huntington-Whiteley was Mentioned in Dispatches. 'Throughout their operations he displayed qualities of initiative and enterprise which was an inspiration to his men and contributed largely to the unit's success,' his citation read.

During Overlord, Huntington-Whiteley led A Troop as part of Woolforce, disembarking on Utah Beach. As they made their way inland they were forced to take cover as bombs rained down around them. As his men crawled across the fields, Huntington-Whiteley walked among them without heed for his own safety, cheerfully telling them, 'Keep your heads down, lads.' His men adored him and enjoyed his light, almost whimsical nature. Patrick Dalzel-Job, another member of Fleming's unit and a soldier of rare panache who himself is considered one of the main inspirations for James Bond, recalled an image of Red sitting on the edge of his bed, lost in reverie, strumming on a banjo and singing Edward Lear's nonsense rhymes as a way of escaping the blood and the madness. *They danced by the light of the moon . . .*

Under the light of the Normandy moon his unit lost 30 per cent of its number, but they fought all the way to Cherbourg and Brittany under continual fire, scouring sites for intelligence – dirty and dangerous work because of mines, enemy snipers and booby traps. But 30 AU was now a crack unit, capable of dealing with whatever was thrown in its path.

That September they arrived in Le Havre to oversee the surrender of a German garrison. The intelligence which suggested that all resistance had either capitulated or been vanquished proved to be inaccurate and Huntington-Whiteley selected seven men to accompany him to the target on the seafront. As they made their way along the beach they encountered small groups of surrendering German soldiers; Red sent two groups back each with two men of his unit, so only he and three others remained in the advancing group. As they reached a small square they came under machine-gun fire and took evasive action. Then another small group of German soldiers emerged waving a white flag. Huntington-Whiteley approached them with a young Marine named Geoffrey Shaw and began to parley.

Suddenly, another group of Germans carrying Schmeisser machine guns rounded the corner. One of his men shouted a warning to Huntington-Whiteley and Shaw, still in conversation with the surrendering Germans. The Schmeisser section opened fire on the entire group, including their own comrades. The two watching Marines ducked for cover behind a hedge. When they looked back once the firing had stopped and the gunners had moved on, the slim spidery figure of Huntington-Whiteley was no longer standing proud. He and Shaw were lying on the ground, both dead.

It was a shocking way for such a brave soldier to die – mown down as he spoke with men who had raised the white flag. The news of his death, at the age of only twenty-four, sent a ripple of shock and bewilderment through the unit. He had seemed invincible. 'A man so beloved of his troop that they were never the same after his death,' remarked one of his men, Jim Burns. According to another, Tony Hugill, the news came 'like a blow in the face'.

Peter Huntington-Whiteley was buried alongside Shaw in Sanvic Communal Cemetery on the outskirts of Le Havre. His father wrote a series of letters to the Special Operations Executive trying to find out the circumstances of his son's death. What he learned prompted a sense of outrage that lived on for many years. In his letter to me shortly before his death, George Chesterton decried the 'cowardly manner' in which his young friend had been murdered.

The Gentlemen of Worcestershire cricket team which toured Berlin might not have been the finest cricket side ever to leave these shores, but as a group of fighting men they take some beating. Certainly in Robin Whetherly and Peter Huntington-Whiteley the side boasted two *Boy's Own* heroes, a pair of the finest and bravest officers the British armed forces have ever produced.

The tide of war had started to turn against Hitler and his troops by 1943. In March that year he lost one of his most trusted cohorts when Hans von Tschammer und Osten died suddenly of pneumonia, aged fifty-five. After a full state funeral his ashes were interred in a shrine in the Langemarckhalle at the Olympiastadion, symbolically linking him with the soldiers who had 'sacrificed' themselves in the battle. Little more than two years later, when the war was over, the shrine and Tschammer und Osten's ashes were removed from the hall. There was no desire to turn the place into a sacred cult site and the idea of a vain, dissolute peacock like Tschammer und Osten, who had been part of a regime that had caused so much unnecessary death and suffering, lying in a 'hall of heroes' was absurd. What happened to his earthly remains is unknown.

As the momentum of war turned, even Felix Menzel's indefatigable ability to organize a game of cricket was brought to an end. During the Battle of Berlin in 1943/44 Bomber Command subjected the German capital to a fearsome aerial assault for six months. For Vice Air Marshal Arthur 'Bomber' Harris the aim was to re-create the firestorm that had engulfed Hamburg in August 1943. During four raids over one ten-night period Bomber Command had dropped nearly eleven thousand tons of bombs on Germany's second largest city and biggest port – 22lb of explosives for each of its 1.75 million residents. The last operation, codenamed Gomorrah, caused a firestorm so severe that it was reported to have melted glass in house windows. The death toll was more than forty thousand, and a million more fled the city. In Berlin during that long winter when the raids were at their most relentless nine thousand people were killed and 812,000 left homeless. But the city survived, albeit with devastating damage.

By the summer of 1944 Harris had been forced to suspend his policy of area bombing to support Operation Overlord and the invasion of mainland Europe. Berliners emerged from their cellars and shelters safe from falling bombs – for the time being. The main threat now was not from the sky but a new terror gathering to their east. The resurgent Red

Army had broken through the eastern front and set its sights on capturing the German capital, seeking to exact a revenge for the destruction and death meted out by German troops as they stormed through the Soviet Union earlier in the war.

Like all males between sixteen and sixty who had not been sent to the front, Felix and Guido Menzel, Franz Hustan and Alfred Ladwig were conscripted into the German equivalent of the Home Guard, the Volkssturm, to whom fell the unenviable task of defending their city from the advancing Russian hordes. Though Goebbels' propaganda still promised victory, the news drifting back to the city from wounded soldiers on the eastern front was grim. Hitler had almost retreated from sight. As its cowardly leaders left Berlin to fight for itself, many of its residents wished for the English or Americans to arrive first, fearing what the Russians might do if they laid claim to the city.

Resources became scarce. Berliners had no option but to grow their own food. The BSV 92 ground, badly damaged by bombs, was turned into makeshift allotments, a process repeated at several other sporting grounds. But amid the chaos and destruction there was some semblance of normality. The Haus Vaterland had remained open throughout the Battle of Berlin, even reopened after its central section was badly damaged during an RAF raid in November 1943. But on 2 February 1945 it was completely bombed out, only its walls left standing.

The Adlon, too, stayed open for business. The foreign correspondents and diplomats who once propped up its bar had long gone, but rich German guests continued to stay there. To its many amenities it added a luxurious bomb shelter, and a vast brick wall was built around its front to stop flying debris damaging the function rooms. Miraculously, given its location, the Adlon escaped major harm and it hosted guests until the final days of the war. It was in the Adlon's restaurant that Eva Braun, Hitler's partner, had lunch in early 1945 with her sister Ilse, who had fled the oncoming Red Army. Ilse warned her sister that Hitler was dragging both her and the German people into the abyss by fighting on even though the war was lost. In reply, Eva told her she should be shot for such views. On 15 April she disappeared into Hitler's bunker where she would die with her Führer.

Six days later the first Russian shells began to fall on the Unter den Linden and the government buildings nearby on Wilhelmstrasse, cutting off water, electricity and gas supplies. Two days after that the SS marched into the Adlon and commandeered it as a makeshift hospital. They painted a huge red cross on its roof so passing bombers would spare it from destruction, though they also mounted an anti-aircraft gun beside it. Then they removed the silk eiderdowns and bedding and Louis XV furniture from the rooms and took them to the cellar – not to be used by those in need but for their own comfort. Approximately two thousand wounded patients were brought in despite scarce medical supplies for the nurses and doctors to treat them with. The senior SS officers didn't care. They were interested only in drinking the contents of the hotel's vintage wine cellar. Like some vision of Hell, drunken generals played the piano, sang and insisted the nurses dance with them to the backdrop of exploding bombs and the moans and groans of the wounded.

Russian troops moved ever closer to the centre of the city, their bombs and shells destroying many of the buildings around the hotel, but still the hotel remained unscarred. On the last day of April, the day Hitler took his own life, the SS men and many of the doctors and nurses fled, aware that the Russians had reached the centre of Berlin after days of ferocious fighting. On 1 May the Russians occupied the hotel. They looted what they could from the patients and staff inside and drank what was left of the wine and spirits. Two days later they set fire to the cellar. When the last few members of staff tried to douse the flames they were threatened with execution. The fire took hold, and in the last desperate hours of Berlin's war the great hotel, which had survived carpet bombing and relentless shelling, was burned to the ground.

The remnants of the German forces had surrendered and the capital was in ruins. A number of the city's landmarks had been destroyed beyond repair. Even the Zoological Gardens in the Tiergarten, visited by the Gents on the last day of their tour, had been devastated: only ninety-one of its 3,715 animals survived.

The end of war did not mean the end of suffering for the residents of Berlin, however. For two awful months afterwards the city was at the mercy of the Russian troops, and mercy was in short supply. Their behaviour was brutal. As Alexandra Richie writes in *Faust's Metropolis: A History of Berlin*, 'By 1945 the Soviet "liberators" had sunk to the depths reached only by the Nazis before them . . . Red Army soldiers were left alone to carry on raping, looting and murdering in an indescribable orgy of violence.' The city centre was a wasteland of rubble, raw sewage flowed in the streets, and corpses were left to putrefy as spring gave way to summer.

Residents resorted to cutting down trees to burn for fuel and there was so little food that many of the two million left in the city were malnourished.

Many Berliners came to despise their Russian overlords and willed the Americans and British to arrive – the very forces that had dropped such fury from the skies and killed so many of their kinfolk. The British, after much effort, finally made it into Berlin on 1 July; the Americans arrived soon after. After several weeks of haggling, Berlin was divided among the four main allies. The British sector comprised much of West Berlin: Spandau, Charlottenburg, Wilmersdorf and Tiergarten.

Berlin cricket was as ruined as the city. Egon Maus, Kuno Lehmann, Gerhard Thamer and the Dartsch brothers had all been killed in action. It appears that Willi Mesecke was also killed, during the battle for Stalingrad. The fates of several others, such as Rolf Zickert and Bruno Behnke, are unknown.* The only members of the younger generation of German players who appear to have survived were Gustav Parnemann and Kurt Rietz, though they had not returned home by the summer of 1945.

None the less, one warm day some time in that month of July a group of British soldiers were stationed at a checkpoint in West Berlin when five German men walked out of

---

* It was a real challenge to discover the fates of the Berlin cricketers. Of the estimated five million men who died in combat more than three million were killed in the Soviet Union and Eastern Europe. As a result of the Cold War, the task of locating their graves and resting places is ongoing. The remains of approximately forty thousand men are dug up and relocated each year – an indication of the staggering losses endured by the Germans as a consequence of Hitler's mania.

the ruins and, to the soldiers' astonishment, asked them for a game of cricket. With Felix Menzel were his brother, Guido, Alfred Ladwig, Franz Hustan and one other unknown cricketer.

The officer was too astonished to speak. Eventually he regained his composure. He wasn't in favour, but his men were. A match was arranged. Where it was held, we don't know; nor is it clear where the equipment came from, though we can assume that no matter how cold it might have got during those last punishing months of the war Felix Menzel would never have thrown a cricket bat on a fire. He foresaw a day when he would need it again. What we do know is that the British side scraped home narrowly as victors despite some very steady and accurate bowling from 'two oldish gentlemen' – doubtless Felix and Guido.

As the game unfolded, the sun on their backs, we can only imagine Felix's conflicting emotions. The war was over and the Nazis had been vanquished; he had survived and he was playing his beloved game once more. But so many people had perished, among them some of his best friends and teammates, that he would have been forgiven for looking around the field and seeing their shadows in the positions where they once stood. But any poignancy he felt did not detract from an enjoyable game. 'We felt in a very good mood,' he wrote later.

To adopt the metaphor used by Home Gordon at the start of war, the grim Test match was over. Evil had been defeated. A new Test had started, and Hope was at the crease.

15

FROM THE ASHES

'THE EFFECT of the Second World War on native German
cricket could be likened to the fate of a precious vase
in a china shop through which something far more violent
than the proverbial bull had passed,' wrote the authors of the
Story of Continental Cricket. The sport had been devastated:
Berlin's sports grounds were in a terrible condition; a
generation of players had been killed; its senior players had
reached an age when it was time to hang up their pads; and
getting hold of equipment presented 'almost insuperable
difficulties'.

On top of all that, chaos reigned in post-war Berlin as the
city tried to haul itself from its knees while the four Allied
powers – Britain, the USA, the Soviet Union and France –
wrestled for control behind a brittle facade of cooperation.
Crime rocketed, the people were in thrall to a growing black
market, and the Soviet grip on the city grew tighter. With its
American, British and French zones, West Berlin became an
enclave surrounded by Soviet-run, communist East Germany.
The Soviets had the greater military presence and controlled
almost all routes in, which meant they administered the city's
supply of food. Stalin's ambition was to subsume the entire
city in the Soviet bloc by forcing the other Allies out. These
tensions culminated in the Berlin Blockade of 1948/49, when
the Russians prevented food from being imported into the
western sectors of Berlin by rail, river or road. In response
the Allies airlifted millions of tons of food into the city to

stop the residents starving. The plan worked. Its success humiliated the Soviets into lifting the blockade and paved the way for the formal division of the city.

But West Berlin remained a small, free island in a vast communist sea. These were not the sort of conditions in which businessmen could prosper, unless they were willing to bend the law or grease the palm of officialdom, particularly communist leaders in the East. While millions flocked into the city after expulsion from parts of Germany under Soviet control, a significant number decided to leave Berlin and head west in search of work and business, or simply out of fear that Stalin would seize total control. Among these emigrants was Felix Menzel.

Though he was in his mid fifties, retiring or winding down was not an option. Like many Germans he needed to work to survive. The post-war trade in Berlin was not to his liking so he moved to Frankfurt, Germany's fifth largest city. We can only speculate why he moved there. Originally it had been chosen as West Germany's political capital, though that decision was changed in 1949 and Bonn was given the honour. It quickly emerged as Germany's main financial centre in the wake of Berlin's division. Frankfurt airport also became the nation's busiest transport hub. There was money to be made there by legal means.

But there was no culture of cricket in Frankfurt. For the early part of the summer Felix satisfied his craving by reading *FuWo* religiously to see how his old friends and teammates were getting on, keeping the cuttings for future reference. Every August he took a month off work and rode the train across East Germany to Berlin to play with them.

Gradually, in his absence, the Berlin cricket scene was

finding its feet. The role of leader had passed from Felix to Kurt Rietz, who had played with little distinction in the series against the Gents. Rietz's enthusiasm for the game almost matched Felix's fanaticism. Before the war he had been a promising football player for the BSV club and had been selected to play for a Berlin representative side. But the match was on a Sunday, when Rietz usually played cricket for Amateure. He mentioned this fixture clash to the selectors. They were aghast. How could he turn down the chance to play for his city in favour of a strange game few of them had heard of? Rietz would not yield. 'On Sunday, I play cricket!' he vowed, and withdrew from the match.

One Sunday shortly after the war Rietz was travelling on a streetcar with his cricket bag on his lap. He was on his way to meet some friends for a practice on one of the few available patches of spare ground amid the rubble. He could sense the man sitting next to him in civilian clothes was itching to speak. Finally he did – in English.

'Excuse me, sir,' he said, glancing down at the bag, 'but do you play this game here?'

Rietz, an Anglophile like Menzel, spoke some English. He smiled. 'Of course. It is cricket.'

'I work for the control commission,' the man explained. 'I would love to play cricket with you.'

They arranged to play a friendly the following Sunday. Rietz managed to gather together a team featuring members of the old brigade such as Franz Hustan, those like him who had survived combat such as Gustav Parnemann, and some younger men who were new to the game. Remarkably, they won. More significantly, from then on they played regular matches against British troops and bureaucrats. Buoyed by this, Rietz restarted the Viktoria 89 cricket team, once again with Hustan; BSV, Germania and Preussen, complete with a visiting Felix Menzel, also rose from the ashes. By the early 1950s the Berlin Cricket League was reborn. A team of the city's best players also played in a league founded by the British Army of the Rhine, filled with teams of troops. The Berliners even managed to win the title on three occasions.

The league's existence drew the attention of the *News Chronicle*'s Berlin correspondent, Bruce Rothwell. He covered the presentation of the league trophy – a bat signed by the 1952 India and 1953 Australia touring teams, as well as the autographs of the England, Middlesex, Warwickshire and Lancashire sides – by British commandant Major General W. P. Oliver. Rietz, the 'Cricket-pioneer' according to Rothwell, admired the bat and told Rothwell, 'We all follow with great interest the Test matches and English county games. All the famous names of English cricket are well known to us.' And what did he think of Len Hutton? 'We think he is the greatest player in the world. We would all love the chance of seeing him playing cricket in his homeland. Perhaps, if we can defeat several more of your local British teams, we will be invited over to play in England.' And hopefully allowed access to The Oval pavilion, he failed to add.

Such a trip never materialized. The Berlin League flourished for a few more years but the decision to increase the length of the domestic football season dealt it a fatal blow. Rather than having two or three months to play cricket, the off-season lasted little more than a month and many players chose to train or rest rather than play cricket. At the same time the Cold War chill forced more players to follow Felix Menzel's example and leave Berlin for West Germany.

Writing in the *Cricket Society Journal* in 1956, E. B. 'Crash' Abbots, a cricket-loving serviceman in Berlin, regarded the long-term prospects for the game in the city as bleak. Too many of its most important players had passed the veteran stage and were on the verge of becoming geriatric. 'The senior representative team still includes regularly at least one player who is well over sixty years of age – he still runs the hundred metres in little over fourteen seconds! – and the average age of the team is consistently above the fifty mark.'

There were only three players who could have been more than sixty in 1956: Felix and Guido Menzel and Alfred Ladwig. Moreover, given that Ladwig had almost lost his feet in the Great War we can assume the sprightly sexagenarian Abbots refers to was one of the Menzel brothers. He also praised Kurt Rietz's dedication to the cause. 'Herr Rietz . . . is working very hard behind the scenes in an attempt to get cricket encouraged in the Berlin schools. If he succeeds, and his persistence certainly merits reward, the future of Berlin cricket will be assured for at least another generation.'

He was unsuccessful. The Berlin Cricket League played its last matches in 1959. A year later the Wall divided the city and the only cricket available to Berliners was the occasional match against British troops. Rietz struggled manfully on, and even managed to coax some players who had defected from East to West to play for his team, but they played on the Maifeld at the Olympic Stadium, occupied by the British Army and off limits for ordinary Berliners. Inevitably, with no cricket to watch and even less to play, the locals drifted away from the game and soon Rietz, by now into his sixties himself, was the sole German in a side of British, Indian and Pakistani expats.

By the end of the war the Major was sixty years old and his playing days were over. But he could still be found on a cricket pitch every now and then: for several years after the war he umpired the Worcestershire v. Combined Services match. He also owned and raced horses at local point-to-point meetings. But his main home was still Worcestershire CC and New Road, where there was no shortage of people willing to stand him a whisky and soda and listen to his stories. He chaired the selection committee for several years before being asked to become the club's president, a role he fulfilled between 1950 and 1955.

The 1950s were the last full decade of the amateur and professional divide in the English game and as always, and despite being very much the amateur, the Major had the respect of the county's pros. He also earned their gratitude: professionals were expected to pay their own costs from their wages, but Young Maurice had opened a dry-cleaning business and the Major negotiated for them a half-price discount to have their kit cleaned.

To his great satisfaction, the Major had the pleasure of watching a successful Worcestershire side in his dotage. From being one of the county game's whipping boys between the wars the side grew in strength and won their first county championship in 1964. Before his death in 1978 at the age of ninety-two the Major was able to witness two further titles, in 1965 and 1974. His passing brought many warm words from cricket lovers across the country, most praising his dedication and persistence between the wars which had saved the club from extinction. Gilbert Ashton, a friend and former teammate, delivered the eulogy at the Major's memorial service at Upton Church. 'And I shall always remember from our cricketing days together the endearing and somewhat quizzical look on Maurice's face when he was giving you just a hint of reproof, or better still, a pat on the back; both always done in the kindliest way.'

The committee room at New Road was well trodden by the Gents. The Major's successor as president was Geoffrey Tomkinson, by now Sir Geoffrey for his services to British industry. He had 'retired' from playing at some stage in his mid sixties, but in name only: whenever Kidderminster were a player short he filled in. The same applied with rugby: he filled in at full-back for Kidderminster RFC at the age of sixty-three. The competitive urge never faded. In 1954 the *Kidderminster Shuttle* reported how Tomkinson was strolling through town when he chanced across a sports day hosted by local carpet companies. He stopped to watch and saw there was a 100 yards sprint for the over fifties, so he entered. Each competitor was given a yard start for each year he was over fifty. Sir Geoffrey won by 15 yards. He was seventy-three. 'I could have won from scratch,' he told the newspaper.

He remained an imposing figure until his death in 1963. Brian Gittins, Kidderminster's historian, remembers him visiting the club shortly before he died to see the new pavilion. One of its attractions was a fruit machine but, in anticipation of Sir Geoffrey's disapproval, it had been unplugged and hidden before his visit (though this austere image is rather difficult to reconcile with the Gent who liked a tour and a drink and enjoyed the entertainments at places such as Haus Vaterland). Sir Geoffrey was the only member of the Gents team to become a published author. He wrote three books, the last of which was on cricket, the self-explanatory *Memorable Cricket Matches*.*

C. S. Anton succeeded Sir Geoffrey as the county club's president to make a hat-trick of former Gents from the 1937 touring side. Cyril Smith also held the role between 1970 and 1972. Smith travelled to Berlin after the war on business. While there he tried to find the doctor who had diagnosed his pneumonia and saved his life. He was upset to learn the doctor had not survived the conflict. Len Pitcher, who was on the Somerset Wanderers tour of 1938, told a similarly poignant story of how the war had devastated the city he knew. Immediately after the war ended he was in Berlin on Army business and tried to trace some of the cricketers he'd played against but couldn't find any. They had all moved or been killed. The only landmark he recognized in the ruins was a tobacconist's where he and his teammates had stocked up on cigarettes. Remarkably, when he walked in the proprietor's wife remembered him immediately. But she warned him not to stay. The shop was in the Russian sector and he wasn't safe there.

Both Cyril Smith and Charles Anton lived long and fruit-ful lives, as did William Deeley, who dedicated much of his

---

* The other two were an entertaining self-published history of his family, *Those Damned Tomkinsons!*, and a slightly less entertaining and rather long-windedly titled *A Select Bibliography of the Principal Modern Presses, Public and Private, in Great Britain and Ireland*.

time to Barnt Green where he is still remembered fondly. He died in 1977. Captain Robert Berkeley had a decent innings too: he survived the war, continued to tend his beloved gardens at Berkeley and Spetchley, and remained Joint Master of the Berkeley Hunt until his death in 1969 at the age of seventy-one. Dickie Williams, as we know, was known to turn up to watch at Stourbridge until his death in 1982. Henry Foley, who withdrew from the touring party for reasons unknown, served as a Temporary Captain in the Rifle Brigade (Prince Consort's Own) during the war, survived the conflict, and died in 1959. Michael Mallinson, who was forced to miss the tour through illness, injury or family commitment, reached the rank of Major in the Essex Regiment and was killed in action near Orsogna in Italy in April 1944. He was twenty-four.

The younger members of the side who survived the war were blessed with longevity. Young Maurice played a few matches without great success for Worcestershire seconds after the war before going into business. He died in January 2005. Peter Terry worked for the family firm, spent a year as High Sheriff of North Yorkshire, and also continued to play with great success for the Yorkshire Gentlemen; he was Vice President right up until his death in February 2006. In an obituary his friend and fellow Gent Roger Hinchcliffe wrote: 'He will be remembered for his sportsmanship, the modesty with which he viewed his own sporting achievements, his charming manner, his undivided attention given in equal measure whether it be to the most humble or the most noble, and not least he will be remembered for his most infectious laugh.'

Peter Robinson died in September 2006. He had gone into

industry, moved to the North-west and sat on the magistrates bench. According to his sons he never played a serious game of cricket again. The highlight of his career remained his trip to Berlin, which means his lifetime career statistics are Innings: 4, Runs: 6, Not Outs: 1, Highest score: 2, Average: 1.25.

In 1995 a German TV crew interviewed Kurt Rietz at his home on Rothariweg in the Tempelhof district of Berlin. He was in his nineties, and rather cruelly they had made him dress in cricket gear for the interview, including a pair of batting gloves. Rietz spoke lucidly and compellingly about his undying love for cricket. Perhaps he had one eye on a comeback. At the end he remarked, 'You can play cricket until you are a hundred. If you are fit.'

At another point he said, 'We had some beautiful matches.' 'Name some!' I shouted at the screen. 'Tell me about Felix Menzel! Tell me about the matches against the Gents! Tell me about trying to play cricket under the swastika! Tell me about the war and the men who didn't come back! Tell me how you revived the game and how it died again!' But none of those subjects were discussed, only the story of how he met a British cricket lover on a streetcar in Berlin after the war and arranged a friendly.

The interview, and the warm words offered by Rolf Schwiete, the late president of the German Cricket Association, belied a myth that grew around Rietz in the 1970s and 1980s. It was said that not only had he retired, depriving the Berlin team of its last German-born player, but that he had then withdrawn from all sporting circles and spent his final years alone, surrounded by a vast amount of memorabilia accrued over several decades, reliving the days of his life.

Rietz died in 1996. I tracked down some old acquaintances who punctured this myth. They confirmed he owned a vast archive of papers, programmes and equipment. No one seems to know what has happened to it. His wife Frieda died before him, in 1994, and they had no children. There was a rumour that the archive had been passed to his carer, a woman named Sabine Döring, but I was unable to find her. I did find Rietz's grave in the Friedhof cemetery, where he's buried beside Frieda, and managed to resist the urge to start digging and see if his memorabilia is buried with them.

Those elusive papers offer the best chance to find out what happened to the members of the Berlin side that played the Gents. Alfred Ladwig lived until his late eighties, as did Franz Hustan. But Felix Menzel was last heard of shuttling between Frankfurt and Berlin in 1956, still desperate to get a game.

EPILOGUE

IT WAS AN early autumn evening and the light was a soft, warm amber glow. There was a chill in the air and darkness was falling quickly, as it always does at that time of year. There were approximately thirty minutes left of what cinematographers call the Magic Hour, and though I wasn't there to take photographs or any moving images it was exactly how I wanted to encounter this scene.

Ahead, to my left, I could just about see the glint of the setting sun on the tip of a golden eagle at the crest of a brick column outside the House of German Sport, preserved as it was three-quarters of a century ago, minus the swastika. Looming behind a row of trees to my right was the Olympic Stadium. I felt a lump in my throat and my heart started to beat more insistently. For a year I'd lived and breathed the Gentlemen of Worcestershire and the cricketers of Berlin; I had met their families and descendants, and in some cases I had seen their writing and read their words. That had been interesting enough, often thrilling. But as I walked down a small street towards the Schenkendorfplatz in the Olympic Stadium complex it felt as if I was actually going to meet these remarkable men at last.

Soon it was in front of me. A giant emerald rectangle – the lush green field of my mind. The bowing trees that surrounded it had been mere saplings back then. The Major and his team were able to see the vast stadium nearby, but now it's obscured. The field is so enormous it has been divided into two full-sized pitches which are used by Hertha Berlin, the city's sleeping giant football team, as their training ground. No wonder the Major had been unable to strike more than three boundaries in an innings of 140.

I stepped over a railing and on to the grass. Behind me I sensed Christian bristle. He had helped me with my research and acted as a patient guide during my visit to Berlin; though we had paid to be inside the stadium complex this was off limits and he wasn't going to join me. But having come this far I wasn't going to waste the chance to walk the same field as the men who had so fascinated me. I've always been excited by the idea of standing on any given spot and thinking, 'A long time ago, something happened here.' In Berlin, like my home London, that feeling takes on greater resonance because recorded history is carved into the landscape. Places bear the documented imprint of their past. I felt that acutely standing on Schenkendorfplatz.

In the distance a couple of bored professional footballers were trudging off the pitch in search of a shower and didn't give me a second look. The turf was like a carpet, beautifully manicured, so flawless it would have made Captain Berkeley gasp with admiration. It wasn't like that in 1937 when the players' boots sank into it up to their ankles. Nor, unlike then, would the wicket have been a problem. A length of matting could be laid on Schenkendorfplatz now and be as flat and true as The Oval.

I stood in the middle of that field and gazed around as the sun dipped below the trees. A few weeks earlier I'd finished another season of club cricket. With each passing year those early autumn evenings seem more poignant. I never know how many more seasons I can and will play, and each year I don't want the sun ever to set. Some men – I'm one, and I know Felix Menzel and Major Jewell were too – can achieve a sense of contentment and pleasant distraction on a cricket field they can rarely replicate in other parts of their life. Cricket is a spell; whatever our worries, whatever ails us, it all recedes when we're on the pitch. Standing there, with the sun on your back, watching this occasionally thrilling, sometimes dull, always compelling game unfold in front of you, the world and its problems can seem a million miles away.

That summer of 1937 the world and its problems surrounded them. The shadows of war were forgotten, or at least pushed to one side. I looked around and I could see them all, like ghosts. The Major and Geoffrey Tomkinson in their fifties, holding back the years, refusing to bow to age and infirmity; the gangly Peter Huntington-Whiteley steaming in, all arms and legs and pace like fire; Robin Whetherly curling his sinewy frame into a crouch behind the stumps; Peter Robinson in innocent awe of it all; Arthur Schmidt wishing he was playing – wishing, perhaps, he wasn't Jewish, the road to Auschwitz stretching out in front of him. The road to war yawning in front of them all.

But, as they always did, my thoughts returned to Felix Menzel. Like many who have devoted much of their life to the sport, I have met some cricket obsessives in my time. Men who haven't missed a match for twenty-five years, who've postponed or cut short weddings, honeymoons and holidays to play. I've even met and interviewed Geoffrey Boycott, and they don't get more obsessive than him. But none of them can lay a batting glove on Felix. Running a cricket team or club requires a certain amount of psychotic devotion. It's always a thankless, time-consuming task. Most of the time you are battling against jealous spouses and other halves, needy children, expanding waistlines, wandering attention spans, chronic injuries and that most intransigent foe, time. However, I've never met anyone who's also had to contend with the most despicable regime the world has seen, the complete annihilation of his city by war, and the death of his friends. And still all Felix wanted to do was play a game of cricket.

What happened to him is, like the man himself, a mystery. As I said, the last record of him comes from 1956. When he finally gave in to the ravages of time and stopped playing is unknown, as is the date he left this mortal crease. Of course he died at some point – James Coldham refers to him in 1983 as the late Felix Menzel – but, like the titular old cricketer leaving the crease in Roy Harper's elegiac song, I'm not quite sure that he's gone. As I stood there in the fading light, the streetlamps starting to pierce the gloaming, Harper's lyrics spun through my mind:

> The hallowed strip in the haze,
> The fabled men and the noonday sun,
> Are much more than yarns of their day.

The story of Felix Menzel, Major Maurice Jewell and the Gentlemen of Worcestershire's tour of Berlin in August 1937 *is* much more than a yarn. It's about war; it's about the enduring beauty of cricket; it's about the madness the sport inspires; and it's irrefutable evidence that even in the most desperate circumstances men and women feel the need to play. Above all it's a story of triumph, of civility over barbarity, of hope over despair.

ACKNOWLEDGEMENTS

I am deeply indebted to a huge number of people who gave up their time to help me in my quest to know more about the 1937 tour to Nazi Germany. Very little was written about it at the time and all of those involved are now dead, but thankfully I was able to track down some of their relatives, ancestors and friends who helped fill some of the many gaps.

John Berkeley, Adrian Hutton, Andrew Perrins, David Williams-Thomas, Graeme Anton, Hugo Huntington-Whiteley, Miles Huntington-Whiteley, the late George Chesterton, Nick Whetherly, Julian and Antony Terry, Roger Hinchcliffe, John Bomford and Sue Cooke, and Nigel Smith all gave invaluable assistance as well as their time, patiently answering my many questions. My special thanks go to Meg Freeman, Sir Geoffrey Tomkinson's daughter, and Michael and Henry Robinson who allowed me access to their family scrapbooks and archives. Paul Clarke of Barnt Green CC, who knew William Deeley, helped me fill in more details of his life, as did Anne Humphries at the Alvechurch Historical Society. Simon Wilkinson of the Upton Historical Society was more than useful in compiling information about Major Jewell, while Melvyn Thompson of the Carpet Museum in Kidderminster went way beyond the call of duty helping me learn more about Sir Geoffrey Tomkinson (and putting me in touch with Mrs Freeman). The Mercian Regiment Museum provided some valuable information about the military careers of Young Maurice Jewell and Tomkinson. Sarah Minney did some excellent research, discovering more about the Army lives of Major Jewell, Captain Berkeley and Sir Geoffrey. I'd also like to thank Penny Hadfield and the staff of the Eton College Archives, and Angharad Meredith, Archivist and Records Manager at Harrow School, for their assistance. More special thanks to Terry Rogers at Marlborough School – without his help the search for some of the tourists would have been infinitely harder.

Phil Mackie of the Gentlemen of Worcestershire Cricket Club was a constant source of information and encouragement. Jon Raby was also kind enough to share a few stories. Tim Jones, Mike Vockins and Norman Whiting are all mines of information about Worcestershire CC and its history and were kind enough to answer my questions, share their expert advice and offer useful avenues for further research. Neil Robinson at Lord's also patiently answered my questions, found references in the MCC minutes to Tschammer und Osten's lunch in 1937, and granted me access to the library. Brian Gittins, fount of all knowledge on Kidderminster CC, shared some fascinating stories and anecdotes about Geoffrey Tomkinson, while Keith Jones of Stourbridge CC did the same regarding Dickie Williams. Jennifer Booth was able to find and share relevant back copies of the Cricket Society's newsletter and journal. Phil Coldham, son of James Coldham, answered all my questions about his father's research and archives, while Simon Pitcher (whose father Len was in charge of the 1938 tour to Berlin)

ACKNOWLEDGEMENTS

was generous enough to send me his father's letters and other memorabilia. Many thanks also to Stephen Eley, Keith Booth, Howard Milton, Jim Davies of the British Airways Museum, Karen Baker of the National Railway Museum, John Russell of the Southern Railway Email Group, Julie Wilde, Philip Bailey of Cricket Archive, Robin Darwall-Smith of Magdalen College, Oxford, Richard Bomford, Don Shelley, Roger Hinchcliffe (who supplied the obituary of Peter Terry), Simon Flavin of Mirrorpix, Isabelle Chaize, and the staff of the British Library in London and the British Newspaper Library in Colindale. Sam Greenhill yielded to my cheeky requests and kindly dug some articles out for me from the *Daily Mail* archive.

In Germany, I was bowled over by the kindness of the staff of the Zentralbibliothek der Sportwissenschaftender Deutschen Sporthochschule in Cologne, especially Elvira Friedrich, who met all my requests for articles with patience and good humour. Oliver Ohmann, chief reporter of *Berliner Zeitung*, was unbelievably obliging and willing not only to meet to discuss the book but also to share his extensive archive of editions of *Die Fußball-Woche*. Speaking of which, the magazine's Ulli Meyer also sent me several copies from its archive which proved vital. Sport historians Heiner Gillmeister and Volker Kluge did what they could to help me discover more about a story, not to mention a sport, that was a mystery to them, as did authors and academics Nils Havemann, Markwart Herzog and Dieter Steinhoefer. Sven Leistikow of Cricket Germany asked around for me and put me in pursuit of the delightful Lu Pfannenschmidt, a friend of Kurt Rietz. She showed immense kindness by inviting me to her home, allowing me to look through her archive

245

of magazines and photographs, and allowing me to eat my body weight in cake. Many thanks also to Kay Gruzdz at the Jewish Museum in Berlin, Hannah Schubert-Dannel of the Central Council of Jews in Germany, Christine Schmidt at the Wiener Library in London, and the members of the online German Jewish SIG for their advice, assistance and suggestions regarding Arthur Schmidt's story. I would also like to offer my thanks to Hans-Joachim-Fieber, Martin Haynes, Elke Fröhlich-Broszat, Cornelia Hoffman at the Deutsche Nationalbibliothek, the State Archives in Katowice, Carina Bitzer, Herr Faraliscz, Nadin Heere and Daniel Gehrke of the TiB club in Berlin. Moving from Germany to Denmark, Ole Christiansen generously shared some stories and photos of the Berlin cricketers' visit to Copenhagen in 1938.

Two people proved such a magnificent help they deserve to be singled out. Simone Pux translated a vast number of articles and reports with great efficiency and accuracy. She knows a good deal more about cricket than she did a year ago. I hope it comes in useful, Simone! Then there's Christian Schoelzel. Without his work on my behalf in Berlin I doubt this book would have been possible. He tracked down articles, TV clips, official reports, books and people with great dedication and put up with my constant queries and exhortations with unyielding patience and good humour. When I visited Berlin he proved to be an informative and fascinating guide, and looked the other way when I started wandering around places where I perhaps shouldn't have been. Thanks, Christian.

That Mark Lucas and the gang at LAW (my agents) do a wonderful job goes without saying, but I'll say it anyway. It was a conversation with Mark that transformed this idea from a possible article into a book, and I'm grateful to my editor Bill Scott-Kerr and his excellent team at Transworld for having the faith to publish it, as well as for their support and enthusiasm.

Finally, I'd like to thank John Stern, editor-at-large of *All-Out Cricket*, for his honest appraisal of an early draft, and my stepmother Irene, whose cricket knowledge was honed over years of watching me play and who also cast a beady eye over the text. Last of all, my love and gratitude go to Seema and the kids, who put up with a distracted, frantic husband and father for a year while I immersed myself in this book. I couldn't do it without you!

BIBLIOGRAPHY

BIBLIOGRAPHY

Ashley-Cooper, F. S., *Cricket Highways and Byways* (George, Allen and Unwin, 1927)

Beevor, Antony, *Berlin: The Downfall 1945* (Viking, 2002)

Birley, Derek, *A Social History of English Cricket* (Aurum, 2003)

Blakeway, Denys, *The Last Dance: 1936 The Year Our Lives Changed* (John Murray, 2011)

Brooke, Robert and Goodyear, David, *A Who's Who of Worcestershire County Cricket Club* (Hale, 1990)

Chalke, *The Way It Was: Glimpses of English Cricket's Past* (Fairfield Books, 2011)

Clark, Sydney A., *Germany on £10* (Nicholson and Watson, 1934)

Coldham, James D., *German Cricket: A Brief History* (1983)

Fisher, Marshall Jon, *A Terrible Splendor* (Three Rivers Press, 2009)

Genders, Roy, *Worcestershire County Cricket Club* (Convoy, 1952)

Gutsmuths, J. C. F., *An Eighteenth Century View of Cricket*, translated by Martin Wilson (Christopher Saunders, 2007)

Haffner, Sebastian, *Defying Hitler: A Memoir* (Phoenix, 2003)

Hesse-Lichtenberger, Ulrich, *Tor! The Story of German Football* (WSC Books Ltd, 2003)

Hilton, Christopher, *How Hitler Hijacked World Sport* (The History Press, 2012)

Hutchins, Roger and Sheppard, Richard, *The Undone Years: Magdalen College Roll of Honour 1939–1947 and Roll of Service 1939–1945* (Magdalen Society, 2004)

Keating, Frank, *Another Bloody Day in Paradise* (Andre Deutsch, 1981)

Kellerhof, Sven Felix, *Berlin Under the Swastika* (Bebraverlag, 2006)

Kershaw, Ian, *Hitler* (Penguin, 2009)

Kircher, Rudolf (tr. R. N. Bradley), *Fair Play: The Games of Merrie England* (W. Collins Sons & Co., 1928)

Labouchere, P. G. G., Provis, T. A. J. and Hargreaves, Peter, *The Story of Continental Cricket* (Hutchinson & Co, 1969)

Larson, Erik, *In the Garden of Beasts* (Transworld, 2011)

Lemmon, David, *The Official History of Worcestershire County Cricket Club* (Christopher Helm, 1989)

Maclean, Fitzroy, *Eastern Approaches* (Penguin, 1991)

McKinstry, Leo, *Jack Hobbs* (Yellow Jersey Press, 2011)

Nutting, David, *Attain by Surprise* (David Colver Publisher, 2003)

Rankin, Nicholas, *Ian Fleming's Commandos: The Story of 30 Assault Unit in WWII* (Faber & Faber, 2011)

Richie, Alexandra, *Faust's Metropolis: A History of Berlin* (Carroll and Graf, 1998)

Root, Fred, *A Cricket Pro's Lot* (Edward Arnold & Co., 1937)

Rother, Rainer (ed.), *Historic Site: The Olympic Grounds 1909– 1936–2006* (Jovis, 2006)

Shirer, William L., *Berlin Diary: Journal of a Foreign Correspondent, 1934–41* (Ishi Press, 2010)

Steur, Claudia and Kutzner, Mirjam, *Berlin 1933–45: Between Propaganda and Terror* (Topographie des Terrors, 2012)

Swanton, E. W. (ed.), *Barclays World of Cricket* (Willow Books, 1986)

Tomkinson, Geoffrey, *Those Damned Tomkinsons!* (Cheshires, 1950)

Walters, Guy, *Berlin Games: How Hitler Stole the Olympic Dream* (John Murray, 2006)

Warner, Sir Pelham, *Cricket Between Two Wars* (Unwin, 1946)

Wilton, Iain, *C. B. Fry: King of Sport* (John Blake, 2002)

INDEX